LEADER

THE JOURNEY TO BECOME THE FORCE YOUR BUSINESS NEEDS TO WIN

CHRISTINE MATZEN

Founder, Oak Street Strategies

LEADER
© 2019 Christine Matzen

All rights reserved. Published in the United States of America. No part of this book may be reproduced or transmitted in any form or by any means, electronic or mechanical, including photocopying, recording, or by any information storage and retrieval system, without permission in writing from the publisher.

Disclaimer: Although I am a leadership developer and strategist, I am not your personal leadership developer and strategist. Reading this book does not create a professional relationship between us. This book should not be used as a substitute for the advice of a competent leadership developer, strategist, or professional business consultant.

This book is not intended as a substitute for the medical advice of physicians. The reader should regularly consult a physician before adopting any new regimens for health.

Readers should consult the professionals in any area that they may require advice or treatment, including medical, psychological, and financial, just to name a few. I recommend that readers consult with licensed, trained, or qualified professionals.

LCCN: 2109909877

ISBN: 978-1-7331789-0-7 paperback
ISBN: 978-1-7331789-1-4 ebook (EPUB)
ISBN: 978-1-7331789-2-1 ebook (MOBI)

Design: Domini Dragoone
Editorial: Sandra Wendel, Write On, Inc.

Publisher: Oak Street Strategies
Website: OakStreetStrategies.com
Email: OakStreetStrategies@gmail.com

TO THE LOVES OF MY LIFE:
DORIAN, JOSEPH, ROWAN,
AND TRYGGR

CONTENTS

Introduction 1

1 What's Leadership Got to Do with It? 5
The Title: Leader
Risk Threshold
What Is Leadership?
The Authentic Leader

2 Make Your Business Something to Yelp About 17
Setting the Tone
Professionalism
Leadership Boundary
Leadership Etiquette
Don't Dirty Your Name
Strategic Partnerships

3 Know What You're Working With 37
Who Is Leading You?
Self-Evaluation
Personal SWOT Analysis
Time Analysis

4 Avoid Quicksand—Plant Your Feet on the Rock ... 47
Define Yourself
Competition
Code for Life
Vision
Vision of Consequence

5 Make It Happen through Action 63
Take Action
Vision to Goal
Alignment
Short-Term Action Plan
Year-End Review
Three-Year Intermediate Plan
Five-Year Trajectory
Evaluating Future Commitments

**6 Avoid the Crash—
Preprogram Your Autopilot Now 75**
Time—A Finite Resource
Minimalism
Capsule Wardrobe
Meal Planning

Outsourcing and Delegation
Hard Work vs. Working Smarter
Multitasking and Balance
A Winning Routine
Spontaneous. Who Me?

7 Boss 101 97
Personal Responsibility
Show up Like a Boss
Personal Development
The Mindset of Excellence
The Art of Mentorship

8 Visit Your Club Med Retreat Every Day 111
Social Connection
Sleep
Nutrition
Exercise
Gratitude
Meditation
Nature

9 Keys to Command 135
Daily Strategic Contemplation
Strategic Response
Command Presence
Hindsight Is 20/20

10 Focus Your Lens Like Paparazzi 149
Feeling Triggered?
The Leadership Lens
Communication
Failure as a Launchpad

11 Speed Bumps, Pot Holes, and Rabbit Holes 161
Use That Knowledge to Win
No One's Friend—Procrastination
What to Do When You Don't Know What to Do
Food for Thought
Technology and the Rabbit Hole
No Excuses the Viking Way
A Final Thought

Acknowledgments 175
About the Author 177

INTRODUCTION

Leadership is an open table, but the entry requires deep personal work and determination. For this reason, many choose not to pull up a chair. If you are ready to become disciplined and driven, then take the open seat at the table.

Today, you begin your new journey to become the leader your business needs to win. The leadership development techniques I offer in this book will allow you to set the vision for your life. There will be no shortcuts, just habits and mindset shifts to help you change your behavior to align with your vision. Have a seat.

Many people come to leadership through chance by opening their own business or having an organic leadership personality. However you have landed in this new role, embrace it. Our society is in need of leadership in every area and in every industry. As you go through the process of development into your position, you will face challenges and defeats.

Keep your eyes focused on the vision that you set—never give in and always move forward.

For me, leadership development has happened over many years. The education that I received through my position as a paramedic was a formative time for me in many ways. My desire to serve others and to give them the highest quality care made me vulnerable. I was vulnerable to the pressures of the corporate model of numbers-driven management. I felt responsible for the community I served and lived in. When we were mandated to constantly stay hours after our shifts, I felt a sense of duty. I felt duty to the community for what I now know is a company's failure to properly staff for the needs of that community—the corporate pressure that I and many other first responders wore like merit badges.

Maybe you too have experienced working in a productivity-based model that thinks of the human provider as nothing more than a productivity machine. You are considered a unit based on utilization hours and overall production alone. The patient, for my situation, became nothing more than a widget to be processed, and the human suffering that we providers carried was a mere inconvenience.

The detriment of care for the patients in this model is vast. Even in other fields, this model seems to be just as concerning, as the discontentment and increased suicide rates extend to many differing industries. The process of getting every drop of productivity remains an unsustainable practice for the human productivity machine. The veracious corporate model relies on the young and unknowing to feed the constant, nonstop motion.

The failure to recognize the needs of the human in the equation leads to a road of broken-down human productivity machines left in their corporate wake. I was, and perhaps you are too, the old model that is cleared for replacement. For us and others like us, these providers have served their purpose and a new shiny model fresh off the press will replace us for a cheaper price. The replacements come with no experience, yet high levels of stamina, and they are ready and willing to fill the void.

This lack of vision of a profits-driven model of management has become the standard in many businesses. There seems to be a failure in the leadership to recognize the "human" in human capital.

I found myself to be a broken leader, as just another productivity machine in the wake. I decided that there must be a better way. I spent years researching and educating myself on healing and lifestyle. In order to move on, I had to heal myself from the severe chronic illness that had engulfed me. I then began to study business and eventually leadership.

This education from the streets and the classroom has allowed me the privilege of developing many strategies to help leaders worth following. In this way, my mission is to change the idea of a profits-only business and to redefine what it means to lead.

Maybe you feel broken or unworthy because you have tried and failed in some area in life. Don't let a perceived failure stop your forward progression. I love a good underdog story, one that proves that a person can drive and overcome obstacles in their path. I believe that those of us who have been broken have a great opportunity for becoming excellent leaders. The process of transformation, although incredibly challenging, allows us to evaluate many areas of our lives. This evaluation will lead to action.

We can take back our power through personal responsibility. The evaluation of our environments and our overcoming of social constructs and social pressure define us as leaders. The confidence we build in our ability to make choices that align with our goals gives us strength to take on new challenges. This is my story—one of challenge, tears, failure, and triumph. This too can be your story so you will become the leader in your own life and beyond.

I feel passionate about helping others to take back their power and to become the leaders that we need to help the next generations to overcome challenges. There is currently a lack of preparation to take the leadership role. I see this becoming normalized in our society. We have lost a sense of personal responsibility and self-reliance. I believe that true leadership that is defined in caring for our teams and encouraging others will change the future. We as leaders have the opportunity to reinvent our lives and business models.

1

WHAT'S LEADERSHIP GOT TO DO WITH IT?

The Title: Leader

Many people are so excited to become entrepreneurs and business owners they fail to recognize that this new role will also give them a new title. Leadership is an important and intense part of the success of any business. Many people believe that once they start a business that they will just become a leader.

Unfortunately, this is not the case. In fact some of the most effective leaders will never even take on a leadership title. These organic leaders can and do exist in every organization. The truth is that people study and work to learn all of the aspects of leadership as their sole endeavor.

The leadership in a business is routinely the reason a business thrives or dies. I encourage all business owners and entrepreneurs to seriously consider making themselves into strategic leaders or hiring an already developed one.

Ask yourself if you are leadership material. I do believe that leaders are made and that you can develop the skills necessary to become a strategic leader. With this in mind, not all people are interested in the responsibility of leadership. Some people would rather focus on their area of expertise and develop deeper in that realm. I believe that there must be a desire to lead and serve others for an individual to be an excellent leader.

If you have done some soul searching and you determine that leadership is just not for you, that's okay. In this case you should look to partner with or hire someone who will fill this role for your business.

There is no shame in recognizing that a leadership position is not for you. This may be a decision you make for now. You may decide to take the leadership role for later. Some decide that taking on the burden of responsibility to others would keep themselves from accomplishing the goals that they have in life. Having self-awareness and the fortitude to follow your life vision is better for you than accepting the leadership role. When you try to force a leadership role, you can put yourself in a position to be unhappy and overwhelmed.

This book will allow you to become a leader in your own life. You will learn strategies to align your life vision with your daily actions. Whether you are ready to take the leadership role or hire it out, take the time to be the leader in your own life today.

If you have decided to take a seat at the leadership table, then let's get started on the path to leadership development and strategy.

Risk Threshold

The idea of entrepreneurship and business ownership is exciting. The fact that you can set the course for your own life is a bonus. With all this excitement comes significant risk in the scenario.

Statistics show that of businesses that were started in the United States in 2014, just over half continued to the fifth year. This is a staggering number of businesses that eventually failed. Approximately 20 percent failed within the first year of the start-up while various others dropped out over the next few years. They cite multiple reasons for failure including lack of capital, loss of need in the market, and lack of leadership.

When determining if stepping out into the world of business ownership is for you, consider if you are prepared to take the risk. Everyone is idealistic that their start-up is going to make it big—whether you're gearing up a tech company, a corner boutique, or a specialty bakery in a strip mall. I believe that you need to feel that passion and excitement to push forward. You also need to be ready for the rocky road that may present itself on your way to success.

Consider ways that you can mitigate some of the risks of failure. Of course, this book will help you develop your leadership skills and perseverance for the long road ahead. As with anything, the information is only useful if you actually apply the knowledge to your life.

Another way to mitigate risk is to not take on large amounts of financial debt by starting slowly and building organically as you make profits. By limiting your financial burden, you can decrease the pressure of a huge loss of money if you decide to change it up or decide maybe that the business is just not for you.

Another possibility is that you scale your business on the side while maintaining your full-time job. Is it possible to take a sabbatical or leave of absence for six months to a year without burning bridges at your current employer? These approaches may not sound like the most exciting ways to get started, but for some entrepreneurs this type of security can and does make the leap to business ownership more realistic.

Whatever path you choose to get started, acknowledge the importance that there is risk with every chance for reward. Take the time to consider what your personal threshold for risk is because this evaluation can save you from a lot of heartache and financial consequences down the road to success.

Your personal risk threshold is something only you can determine based on your fear of failure. What will happen if you fail? Will you be able to just move on and find your next opportunity? Will you be completely devastated at the loss?

Some leaders are able to disconnect emotionally and just learn from the experience. They take the newfound knowledge, move on, and make the next business a success. For others, they feel emotionally devastated and find fear in trying again. Please take your personal risk threshold into consideration when making your entrepreneurial plans.

What Is Leadership?

Leadership is a living, breathing action of a small subset of people. Leadership is a true caring about others and an internal strength that is radiated to those around you. Leadership is the ability to influence others who would follow you even into the most difficult situations.

The characteristic that defines an excellent leader is that they always strive to bring out the best in the people they lead and interact with. They have the ability to strategically plan and execute when they need to. They apply a mindset of excellence in everything they do. They also recognize team success and take complete responsibility for failure.

Think of an accomplished leader in your life. Do you notice that when you are with them you strive to do your best? Maybe you hold yourself to a higher standard or recognize areas that you want to improve in your life. This is a beautiful consequence of excellent leadership.

I believe that leaders are made, and many will develop the skills and the internal strength to grow into the true leadership roles in life. Leaders must be disciplined and prepare for the "hard calls." You can never predict the challenges that could arise on your watch, so a dedication to lifelong learning and critical thinking is required.

Think of the industry leaders in your realm who had to take the lead during our last market downturn in America. Practically overnight there was a financial crisis, and businesses that the day before were flourishing were now in a tailspin. The leaders that had an emergency plan with financial reserves and a calm and steady strategy were able to weather the storm. Many leaders were not able to adjust, businesses went under, and employees and communities were forever changed.

There can never be enough emphasis placed on the concept of lifelong learning and self-evaluation in the leadership position. The opportunities for learning in our current technological age are limitless. This is an exciting time for leaders to develop themselves while pushing forward through innovation and information. The discipline of acquiring knowledge and the application of that knowledge in your life can be the catalyst for leadership success.

We need strong leaders in our society. With this book and my workshops, I want to develop leaders worth following. We need to find our personal strength and be willing to put in the hard work that is required to make a meaningful impact in our lives—and in the lives of those we lead. I want leaders to design lives that they love, which are full of choices that minimize regrets.

Leadership is a skill that can be developed over time. Even those who have many inherent leadership skills can only develop wisdom through experience. Developing intuition and strategic thinking takes time and opportunity. There are no shortcuts to exceptional leadership. You have to actually show up and put in the work. Oh, you'll make mistakes and missteps along the way. I believe that leadership is a life's work—something that you can continue to develop in different ways for your whole life.

Many people believe they will be given a title and, all of a sudden, the magic of CEO behind their name will turn them into a leader. That somehow the power of the title will garner them respect from others. Nothing can be further from the truth. All too often these are the businesses that fail or go through huge growing pains due to the lack of strong, steady leadership. Although employees may be forced to follow your directives, respect in leadership is earned.

Many different leadership styles exist. Some leaders are charismatic and others are quiet warriors. There is no difference with such dissimilar personalities in the level of success they can have as leaders. They employ different techniques and tactics to be effective in delivering their vision. For a leader to be truly effective, they must be authentic to their true self.

If you care for the people you lead as if they were family, and show compassion easily and anger with restraint, this will lead to significant team cohesion and loyalty. As you become the leader in your own life, you should strive to be true to your authentic personality and principles. You may hear many voices throughout your day. None will be louder or more frequent than your own. Use this information wisely as the leader in your own life and business.

The Authentic Leader

For many, leadership is a default title—one that they did not initially set out to accomplish. As you develop your personal leadership style, it is important that you stay true to the person that you are. No two leaders are the same, and there are many different ways to lead that are effective. People tend to respond negatively to those who try to be someone or something that they are not, and leadership is no different.

If you are a charismatic person, let that be your strength. If you are a creative, nurturing person, stay true to that quality. Learn to use techniques that incorporate your personality and skills.

When determining how you will lead, take into account that how you treat your employees will impact how they behave. If you use a strict policy and treat the adult employees like children, then expect that they will behave in such a way. Employees that feel devalued and micromanaged often times will not rise to the occasion under that leadership. Strike a balance to the standards that you expect and the action of your employees.

Caution to new leaders about their newfound power: A sense of overbearing power can come from new leaders. This is usually fueled more from the immense sense of responsibility that they now face. Until you are in your leadership position, it can be easy to speculate how you would have handled a situation differently. But nothing can prepare you for the day that the weight is placed on your shoulders. There is a definitive change when you realize that you are now completely responsible.

Leaders do not routinely desire to be bossy. The realization that you are now completely responsible can be a shock to some. In this case, I try to remind leaders to focus on the role of service to their employees—try to make sure that your employees have everything that they need to do their jobs. Make sure that your leadership plans are well developed and communicated. This planning and preparation can help to overcome the stress of ultimate responsibility.

Employees have a keen sense to recognize the leaders who have the best intentions toward them. This is not about letting employees take advantage of you as a leader. You want to be clear by following and enforcing the company guidelines and policies. This is about being caring and compassionate to the people on your team. When your employees feel valued, they will respect you. There is really no incentive plan or punishment metric that can produce the same result as just really doing right by your employees.

Hire people who respond well to your leadership style and standards. This is a priority when expanding your team. Hiring employees should be an in-depth procedure. You are bringing on people who will be representing you and contributing to your workplace culture. This is incredibly important to your growing business. Take your time when bringing on new employees. On the other hand, be quick to remove an employee who is creating a negative environment.

Consider each applicant as an individual by looking closely at the skills they will be able to bring to the table. Employing people who have different skill sets and work well with others allows you to build your team cohesion.

When it comes to choosing the right employee, look deeply at the applicant's qualifications as well as their attitude. Pay careful attention to their level of respect and initiative. Highly qualified applicants are out there and come in all shapes, sizes, and age groups. Spend the time to get to know the applicants a bit better because this will define the people who are the cream of the crop. Respect and personal responsibility are nonnegotiable for me when I look to partner or hire. If a new employee is coachable, I have confidence that they can learn other skills that they will need in the workplace.

KEY INSIGHTS

- Leadership is essential to win in business; become a strategic leader or hire a developed one.
- Leadership is a skill that can be trained with hard work and determination.
- Leadership should bring out the best in ourselves and the people we lead.
- Risk is inevitable in life and business; evaluate your own personal risk threshold and plan accordingly.
- Leadership style should be developed in alignment with your genuine self.
- Hire employees that align with your leadership style and the core values of your business because this practice will lead to success.

2

MAKE YOUR BUSINESS SOMETHING TO YELP ABOUT

Setting the Tone

If you set the highest standard for yourself every day, your example will change the culture of any workplace. Leaders who expect the most out of themselves by encouraging growth and value from their team will garner loyalty. This loyalty will help to form the strong team environment from those they hire.

Leadership will set the tone not only for your organization but for your life. The most effective form of leadership is through example. How you present yourself and the way that you behave in every situation will be emulated by those around you. For instance, the leader who gossips or makes excuses for not meeting goals gives the green light to those behaviors to the rest of the staff. Never expect your staff to hold themselves to a higher standard than the one that you hold for yourself.

What a leader tolerates will continue to grow. There can definitely be a balance in leadership. Although you do not want to micromanage or limit innovation or development, it's reasonable to want your employees to take ownership and feel valued while still adhering to the company vision and core values. You also do not want to foster bad behavior.

When you identify bad morale or behaviors that are not in alignment with your company culture or leadership standards, end that behavior immediately. Negative behaviors such as gossiping, bullying, lying, or mean-spirited customer service, just to name a few, can quickly degrade the work culture. A happy and fulfilled culture grows stronger through time and accomplishment. Unfortunately, truly one bad apple will ruin the bunch. Even one employee who spreads bad behavior and discontent can change the entire work environment.

You can read about the many different leadership philosophies and styles in a wealth of business and leadership books. Having worked in many different environments and with differing leadership styles, I formed my opinion of leadership. My education and my continued work with leaders has only bolstered this opinion.

I have come to see that the leader who believes that they are part of the team, not above it, tends to develop greater respect and loyalty from their team. This believing that they are part of the team and seeing their employees as people and valued teammates instead of just numbers changes a leader's commitment and care of the team. I believe the best leaders are first solid teammates.

The leaders I want to develop are people who care about others. They want to build respect and value in their businesses. They want to be examples of integrity and courage to those around them. This is not about becoming the CEO of a large company that has no problem laying off thousands of employees, while the next week spending millions for the executive team to vacation in the Bahamas.

This is about the business owner who would look for solutions to maintain as many jobs as possible during a crisis. A business that thinks of the employees like family and works together to overcome challenges. Although big business does have its place in our global economy, small to medium-sized businesses offer many opportunities for success as well as a change from profit-driven numbers management.

Why do we continue to spread this idea that it's not personal, it's just business? I find this idea infuriating. It should be personal for a leader to see the employee base as a team or a family of sorts. We should be working to enhance the lives of those on our team while also producing worthwhile products to our customers. Do leaders really expect that employees that are treated as a number will show loyalty to the company or customers? What is the tone that we want to set for our organization?

We need to reevaluate how we do business. The concept that the homogenized corporate model in every city is the testament to a successful business is something we need to evaluate moving forward. Is bigger really better? We need to shift our perspective of what it means to be a prosperous business, and, as the leader, you have the power to do this.

You can choose to share more of your profits with the employees and encourage longevity in them. As your business grows, mentor and educate so that you can promote within the business. Make giving back and respecting your community an important part of your business philosophy.

I firmly believe that the businesses that treat their employees with respect will see a complete shift in the loyalty they receive, not only from their employees but from the customers as well. When you treat your employees well, and they value your business and leadership, they will in turn treat your customers well. Employees are the face of your company. The employees' sense of value can quickly be conveyed to your customers and community.

Change your perspective on how much profit is enough. Pay your employees a higher salary and hire employees who align with your company values. Take your time to hire well-qualified applicants who have an eagerness to do well. Search for employees who are coachable and excited to be part of a company like yours.

I know these may seem like radical ideas when you are first starting out. I encourage you to take your time and grow slowly. As you progress and take on more employees, think through what type of employer and leader you want to be. Do you really want the lowest-paid, high-turnover employee as the foundation of your business? We can and should do better.

We need to stop looking at profit alone as our guidepost for leadership—the type of business that depersonalizes the individuals they employ. A CEO who is willing to do anything for profit is management, not leadership. These are two quite different philosophies, and I am not interested in profit-driven management.

Sadly, this model has continued to develop under the guise of fiduciary responsibility—the idea that the corporation has a responsibility (a duty) to be increasingly profitable to the investors. Although I agree that a business has a responsibility to the investors in maintaining a level of profitability, we seem to miss the forest for the trees. The fiduciary responsibility extends to the corporation as a whole, which should include the backbone of any organization—the human capital.

We as leaders of corporations should be responsible to our employees by paying them a responsible wage and giving them access to healthcare and retirement benefits. This should be the standard among profitable companies. The fact that the going rate is the bare minimum imposed by the government is a travesty. Posting record profits in the billions while your employees qualify for food stamps and government-subsidized healthcare should be boycott worthy.

I am not talking about the start-up companies that can truly afford to pay only minimum wages to employees because they are not yet profitable. That is a completely different story.

In the race to the top of the corporate model, we seem to have lost sight of what it means to be a sustainable longevity-based corporation. We no longer see corporations that consider having the best workplace and packages as the norm. We have allowed these companies to turn profits on the backs of their employees, all under the protection of fiduciary responsibility and profit-based management.

Social pressure from communities should disallow this type of management from succeeding. This social pressure with strong leadership in new company models could help to elevate the small and medium-sized local businesses.

Do you remember what towns were like before the homogenized corporate chain model took over? When every town that you visited did not include the standard Panera, Panda Express, Starbucks, and Target. When you traveled around, not every town had the same restaurants and stores. You could find the cute cafes, the family restaurants, the interesting local bookstores, and kids' toy stores. These small businesses offered something different with the flair of the owner and the sense of the community at their core.

I remember our small California town where I was raised. Owners and employees knew the details of every product they carried in these small stores. My parents owned a beautiful small flower shop. My mother took such pride in the arrangements that she made. The detailed customer service that they gave was often comforting to families as they planned for a funeral service. Now you can just order a pre-made arrangement online to be drop-shipped for the casket. No face-to-face communication or attention to detail or individuality required.

This loss of the personal touch seems to exemplify the loss of connection that continues to grow in our society. Our corporate greed and the elevation of certain business models have changed the face of the business market and sent most manufacturing overseas.

Don't misunderstand, I love profits and businesses that do well. I believe that you can have wonderful business models that are fiscally responsible. Leadership worth following treats their employees well and cares about the community where they operate. You can maintain your fiscal responsibility to the company without the need for the largest profit, at the expense of your employees.

We need to encourage the small and medium-sized businesses where everyone knows your name, and we all rise or sink together with the tide. We need to reinvigorate a sense of community and caring in business and beyond. In short, we need to redefine ourselves as leaders and change the tone of business.

Professionalism

Start today with professionalism even if you are a one-person show. When you always hold yourself to a high level of professionalism, others will follow. There is an old saying about avoiding the appearance of impropriety. This is an excellent guide to go by when determining if something is unprofessional or unethical in your work environment.

A lot of attention these days is given to harassment and inappropriate behavior in professional settings. Set strong boundaries with employees and require open-door policies, which will help to avoid any untoward situations.

In any work environment we should maintain an open-door policy. There should also be a chaperone policy in place when delicate meetings are necessary to respect those involved and to maintain the appearance of impropriety. These may seem like old-fashioned suggestions. In the current culture with changes in the relationship of the genders, this is a way to ensure the integrity of all involved. Take the time and effort to protect all individuals; this is an ethical responsibility of leadership.

When creating your work culture, recognize the importance of setting standards for what will be acceptable in your work environment. Create a culture of respect and inclusivity, which is important to allow for innovation and team cohesion. Team-building exercises and company metrics that measure effort and teamwork, not just outcome, can set up a winning environment.

As the leader you need to take the time to make sure that you have clearly defined your business mission, vision, and core values. Just as the personal statement, code of life, and vision are essential for building your life as a leader, these are essential qualities to building culture and direction in your business. Remember to make sure that your actions as the leader remain in alignment with your business mission and core values.

Nothing degrades the morale of your employees faster than a leader who acts with disregard for the foundations of the business. Take, for instance, a hospital that has a mission to give quality care to patients while providing a healthy work environment to hospital employees. If the hospital requires the providers to care for more patients than they can do safely or requires extra hours on a regular basis, the morale of the providers will easily be degraded and patient care will suffer. The negative attitude will build within the providers as their needs are not met on a routine basis. This negative morale will spread like wildfire to all hospital employees.

These are all nonverbal ways in which you as the leader have the opportunity to communicate value and respect to yourself and your employees.

Treat customers and business contacts with the same level of professionalism in alignment with your mission and values, which will allow you to build respect in the community. Look for opportunities where you can continue to communicate value and care of your community to build brand loyalty and increase revenue.

You can find many ways to achieve this mission. Use some of your profits for example, to donate to cleaning up a city park for children. Have you and your employees take to the streets with paint cans and cover graffiti. Give back in a visible and caring way to increase the value of your business in the community where you operate. A transparency on the way that you take care of your employees via higher wages, profit sharing, day care, or any other incentive can encourage the customers that their patronage is helping to make this possible.

Many community members are willing to pay a bit more for a product or service knowing that the money is being put to superior use, especially when your product or service is top-notch.

A special note to leaders about romantic relationships in the workplace; I encourage all leaders to have a defined policy around any romantic involvement within your workplace. The rules for these sorts of interactions should be detailed and clear before you hire on any additional staff.

Although everyone loves a Romeo and Juliet story that unfolds in front of their eyes, such office romances don't always lead to happily ever after. When the relationship turns to be more like Glenn Close in *Fatal Attraction*, you do not want your company culture to be in the middle of the battle. Make sure that you discuss your dismissal guidelines in the event that you are required to enforce the policy. Transparency can make for a lot less awkwardness if this relationship becomes an issue for you and your corporation.

I continue to encourage workplaces to include spouses/partners and children regularly in the work environment. Spouses can easily be invited to working dinners or lunches. Have a family open-door atmosphere, which will contribute to more professional and ethical interactions. We want to encourage family and friend connections for our employees as well as for ourselves.

Leadership Boundary

They say that it is lonely at the top, which can be true if you do not cultivate a group of friends. While you maintain a professional boundary in the work environment, which is incredibly important, have a circle of equals outside of your workplace that will help you keep the lines drawn.

There is the need for a professional boundary at all times with your employee base. The constant oversharing and need to be vulnerable has led to some uncomfortable and compromising situations for leaders. We live in a reality-TV world where it has become the norm to share deep emotional vulnerability with the world (think social media here too). In an area where you are the leader, respect the importance to be true, honest, and occasionally vulnerable. On occasion showing that you may not have all the answers or that you are having a tough moment allows your employees to connect with you as a person.

This vulnerability is far different from feeling as if you need to tell your employees every detail from your personal life. Opening yourself up in that way in a situation where you may have to fire or discipline someone will put you in an uncomfortable position. Maintain a professional yet friendly boundary. This is always the best policy when dealing with employees.

Employees, at times, will overshare or become too comfortable with airing dirty laundry in the workplace (or on social media). Again, you want your employees to feel comfortable and supported, but if you allow your employees to create a negative gossiping environment, it will lead to a degradation of professionalism in the workplace. Discontentment and gossiping can spread through an office or shop or warehouse like wildfire. This type of negativity can be difficult to turn around.

Make friends with other leaders and people who are pushing toward excellence, outside of your workplace. You will have people to share and learn from. These people can be honest with you and push you toward meeting your goals while you can do the same for them. Keep this circle of friends tight. They are the friends with whom you can share the details of your life and your thoughts without making yourself vulnerable in the work environment.

Make sure that your friends are willing and capable to give you their true opinion when you need it. You do not want shallow friendships with others who just tell you what you want to hear to keep from hurting your feelings. As a leader you need a tight group of friends or family members where you can go and know that you will be respected and given truth, and in return you will do the same for them.

Having this group of friends and family will help you to maintain your emotional temperance and professional boundary while at work. Often new business owners and entrepreneurs spend so much time in the workplace that they fail to nurture these outside relationships.

When you lose touch with your friends, such loss may lead you to oversharing and becoming vulnerable to your employees. Although it can be gratifying to be friendly with teammates, you do not want to overshare with your subordinates. This can make for awkward situations in the workplace and can make you, as a leader, feel as if you are unable to correct unacceptable behavior from employees who know personal details about your life.

When determining whether to share a vulnerability in the workplace (to discuss a divorce or child using drugs or medical condition), decide if the information is common knowledge and for public consumption. For instance, maybe you were previously married and everyone knows that you are divorced. This situation may make you feel vulnerable, but it is a part of your history. You have come to terms with the impact of it in your life. Sharing this tidbit is not compromising you in any way.

On the other hand, if you are married and going through a difficult term in your marriage and you are unsure if you will remain married, this information is the type that you would want to keep for your inner circle. Raw emotional vulnerabilities that you do not know what the outcome will be can make for uncomfortable situations for a leader in the workplace. Oversharing personal details is different than acknowledging situations that you have faced in life that have helped to form you as the person you are today.

Maintain your professional boundary in the workplace while you foster the close relationships with friends and family, which will serve you well in your leadership role.

Take on a mentor or coach in some area of your life. Once you start to operate at a high level and you are just looking to take it to the next level is the ideal time to take on a coach or mentor. Mentors and coaches can help you to keep your focus and to push through difficult plateaus in different areas of your life. Amazing coaches and mentors are worth their weight in gold. Take your time to hire coaches and mentors who have the right level of education and experience to help you.

Make sure that they are walking the walk that they teach so that you can have the best possible experience.

Leadership Etiquette

True leadership stands out in a crowd. Show kindness, respect, and courtesy to others, which will not only change the way you feel, but it will encourage those who interact with you.

Leaders worth following recognize the importance of following a code of behavior in everyday life. Whether you are in your leadership role or out in the general public, here are some specific areas to which a leader should pay attention.

Courtesy: For instance, elderly people who may need your seat on the subway or a mother with a small child who could use a hand. As a leader, you are strong and capable, and these simple signs of respect and kindness can go a long way. Even the kind act of holding the door for someone can demonstrate attention to detail and respect. Leaders, build your command presence through courtesy and kindness.

Politeness: I love the sound of "yes, ma'am" and "yes, sir." This clearly shows that you are comfortable and strong in yourself as a leader. Knowing how to be polite to others with whom you interact is a gift. Those who respect themselves and have confidence have no problem showing politeness.

Eye contact: Eye contact and smiling can be effective tools for communicating trust and establishing connection with your subordinates or the general public. You should make it a point to make eye contact with others throughout the day. A well-placed smile can make someone's whole day. This is an awesome opportunity to let your leadership etiquette shine through.

I challenge you to show your leadership style and begin practicing these simple rules for behavior in everyday life. Strength and confidence are well demonstrated through leadership etiquette.

Don't Dirty Your Name

When you are the leader, have strong moral principles and be honest because this is incredibly important to the lasting success you want to strive for. Success is built through giving what you promise on a regular basis.

"Don't dirty your name" was a regular saying from my grandparents whenever we left the house for work. The idea was that, when people heard your last name, they should know that they could trust that the job would be done well. That your name and your word were enough to know that others could trust in you.

The way to build this name for yourself and your business is to deliver on your promises. If you say that you will show up ready to go at a specific date and time, be there. Don't over-promise and then hope that you can get a task done. You want to build the reputation for your business that people can trust you.

Have integrity in business because this will allow you to develop working relationships with business partners. The customers that you interact with will likely feel valued and respected and in turn develop brand loyalty. When people interact with businesses and people of integrity, they spread that name to everyone they know with enthusiasm. A word-of-mouth recommendation or review can be a strong determining factor when people decide to choose a business to partner with or buy from. Yelp doesn't have the corner on reviews.

When businesses lack integrity, the word that is spread can be measured tenfold. When you hear a negative story or review, it can quickly change the perception of the business. One negative review can diminish many positive reviews, especially if the complaint revolves around a lack of integrity of the business. Social media have made bad reviews on such platforms as Yelp almost death to a business.

Strategic Partnerships

As the leader of your business, you will forge the relationships with the suppliers and partners you work with. This can be a fun and exciting opportunity to increase business success or outsource your workload.

Whenever you are taking on a strategic partner or hiring a business, I recommend that you do your due diligence. Take the time to investigate the company and talk to the leadership. Ask for personal references or look at reviews. You can find many reviews with the Better Business Bureau, Yelp, and Facebook, just to name a few resources.

We live in a technologically advanced age with information galore, but be careful to vet the source of information before acting on it. Work with companies that align with your values and mission to achieve your business success.

Price is not the best measure for choosing these companies. Usually you will find that if you go by financial bid alone, you get what you pay for. You want to make sure that you are aligning with businesses of integrity that will do a high-quality job and provide you with excellent customer service.

Choosing the wrong strategic partnerships can put the

success of your business at risk. Aligning with companies that do not value your business may lead to missed deadlines or mistakes that impact your business goals. These businesses can cost you time, money, energy, and frustration. Don't fall into the trap of basing these partnerships on the financial bottom line. This is not about buying something that is super expensive. Make sure that the partner you work with will serve you well and be fiscally responsible. The more you look into other companies, you will get better at evaluating owners that want to do the best job possible, and it matters to them on a personal level.

Take the time to join business associations in your local community. Attend meetings and get-togethers through the local chamber of commerce. These are excellent opportunities to talk with fellow business owners in your area. You may also find opportunities to work with other industries to build your customer base.

Your competition may be your strategic business partner. Although there is a small subset of business models that still work off a direct competition model, you may find opportunities to differentiate and work together. Many of the new leaders recognize the concept that the incoming tide raises all boats.

Take the time to get to know and evaluate the competition that is in your business genre. Is there a way that you can differentiate from the other businesses and then work together in shared ways to drive up customer awareness? Some hotels will differentiate by becoming family friendly while others will become the boutique adult-only option.

Businesses can work together in many ways to increase revenue for all involved. For instance, many hotels and restaurants will work together on advertising campaigns or packaged deals to drive tourism to their towns. They know that working together increases the likelihood of business success for all the different industries in their towns. I think of the "Magnolia Movement," as I call it in Waco, Texas. The success of Chip and Joanna Gaines in fixer-upper homes and home décor has allowed for significant tourism and growth within this small community. They have purposely worked directly with local business to encourage growth in that area.

Look for new and innovative ways that you can work together to increase the business in your community. Just make sure that you take the time to vet the other business owners and ensure that they are in alignment with respect and integrity.

KEY INSIGHTS

- Set a high standard for yourself as the leader, which will encourage others to adopt high standards for themselves.

- Leaders should care about their employees and foster a team environment.

- Leaders are ethically bound to create a safe workplace; this includes open-door and chaperone policies.

- Create a healthy leadership boundary in the workplace. Foster friendships and mentors where you can maintain vulnerability and accountability for yourself out of the purview of your employees.

- Show strength as a leader with the application of leadership etiquette.

- Have integrity in the way that you operate your business. Develop a strong work ethic and a sense of responsibility to build brand loyalty.

- Create strategic partnerships with other businesses to increase your opportunities for success.

3

KNOW WHAT YOU'RE WORKING WITH

Who Is Leading You?

Now that you are ready to take on the leadership position, consider who is leading you. Remember that leadership is influence in any area of your life. Where is your influence coming from? Is the information and influence that you have in your life helping you to develop into the person you strive to be?

Take the time to evaluate the people or ideas that are influencing you in your life. Look to remove the influences that will not encourage you to reach your goals as a successful leader. Often leaders find that they need to disband with the status quo of the population and march to the beat of a different drummer.

Change the beat in your life and become protective over the information and people that you allow to influence you, which will help you to make changes. These changes that you need to make in your day-to-day life may be subtle. Subtle changes can be powerful in helping you to become disciplined and focused toward your vision.

Consider even the simple acts such as what you watch on television or what books you are reading. Remember that what you focus on and listen to will change your perspective and influence your daily actions. Try reading books from leaders in the industry where you would like to find success. Inspiring and powerful biographies are available and can be used to mentor you and foster growth on your journey. A leader can use these types of information in a positive way to inspire and excite them personally, even during times of struggle.

Sometimes you need to look closer at friends or family who may not be supporting your positive changes in life. These types of influences might not be helpful to your development as a leader. Surround yourself with family and friends who show concern, when warranted, and give encouragement for you to step out and take opportunities. This type of support will increase your drive toward success.

Self-Evaluation

Become the best leader you can, which begins with knowing where you are starting from. You cannot begin to change and have progress until you acknowledge where you are now. I like to keep life simple, so I recommend a SWOT analysis—among the many different types of assessments that you can do to evaluate your life and purpose. The SWOT analysis was originated by Albert Humphrey of Stanford University in the 1960s.

Yes, anyone who has attended business school is thinking you want me to perform the same analysis I learned for my business on my own life? Absolutely, this is an amazing and simple assessment that not only allows you to see the areas that you need work on, but it also gives you a look at the areas where you are doing well. This process allows you to see how you can mitigate the negatives with the positive. You can offset any threats with opportunities, and that is the right place to start.

When performing your SWOT analysis of your strengths, weaknesses, opportunities, and threats, try to be as detailed as possible. Remember you cannot change what you do not acknowledge.

Let's get started with the SWOT evaluation. In the first two sections we will look at the areas within ourselves that impact our lives and progress:

> **Strengths:** Take the time to write out all of your strengths that apply to your life. Maybe you have excellent communication skills, a supportive spouse, a strong education. Maybe you have awesome people skills and can sell anything. You get the picture. Let it flow with all that you have to offer yourself and those around you.
>
> **Weaknesses:** List all your weaknesses or the areas in your life that are holding you back. Maybe you have

a cluttered home and feel overwhelmed. Maybe you lack skills or knowledge that you need to push forward. Maybe you want to lose fifty pounds and you feel as if that weight is holding you back from completing your mission. This area should be as detailed as you can get.

Let out all those emotions, frustrations, and feelings of being stuck onto the paper. Once you have them down, you will have the opportunity to make changes for your life to improve. Don't let this section take you off course. Just acknowledge that you have areas to work on to improve your future.

In the next two sections we will list the opportunities and threats that are outside of our personal selves. Take time to do some research and brainstorm the many opportunities that you can use to your advantage. The internet can be a target-rich resource for finding opportunities that you can leverage against your threats.

Opportunities: List anything that could be used to your advantage, even if you may not need it right now. This is a place where you can gather extra resources that may be strategically put in play depending on personal challenges you may face in the future. Maybe your local gym is having a three-month free special or your local college is hosting a leadership class in the evenings. Think of this section as any outside resource that you can use to enhance your life and capabilities.

Threats: Write out anything that may threaten your ability to meet your goals. This can be any outside influence that may create a challenge for you to overcome. Maybe you are having a difficult time finding day care for your children. Maybe business colleagues are unsupportive of your weight loss goals and are always bringing in cakes and brownies to the office.

Once you have all of the SWOT sections complete, take time for some simple analysis of how you can mitigate your weaknesses and optimize your strengths. This process will give you a good idea of the areas in your life that need some improvement and an opportunity to come up with solutions for the threats that you currently face.

In the following example you can see that if you have a spouse who is willing to help you meal plan, you can easily bring food to work that keeps you full and happy so that your coworkers' pastries cannot tempt you. There, you have mitigated the threat that they presented to your success.

Day care can be an overwhelming situation as you want your children well cared for. There can be many solutions including family members or local childcare centers. I often will tell working moms to collaborate with stay-at-home moms. These are awesome situations that can be a win for all involved. A stay-at-home mom could provide day care and earn some money from home. Your child would be well cared for, and in return you could pay less than a care center would require for exceptional care. These out-of-the-box strategies can be excellent resources for all involved.

I recommend that every ninety days you repeat or review your SWOT analysis to stay on top of any changes that may be coming your way. You will see that this will align with the timing of your action plan that you will develop later. Doing all of this evaluation at the same time allows you to add in any new planning steps that may be required to help you meet your goals.

Personal SWOT Analysis

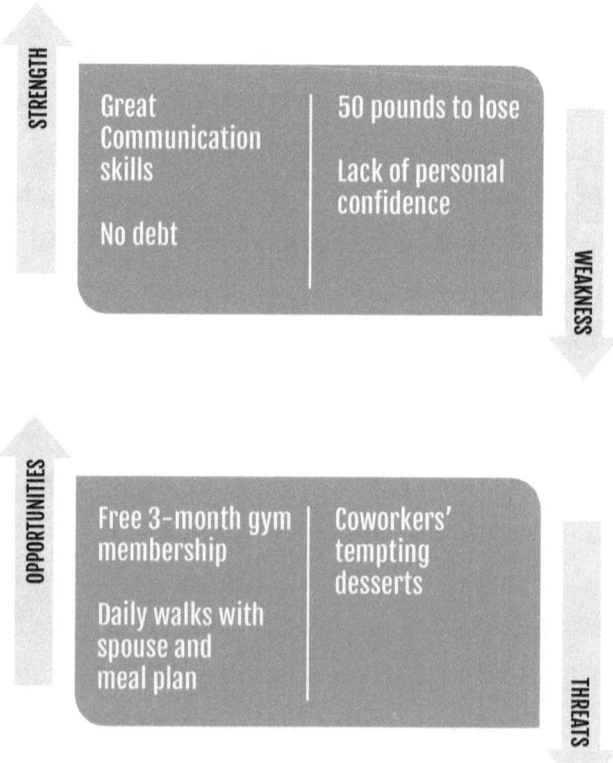

Time Analysis

The second self-evaluation method that I recommend is a simple time analysis. Our days are now completely bombarded with distraction and marketing. These distractions can be insidious in the way that they eat up our time and our ability to stay focused.

The observations of the way that the human brain has been affected by these technologies is staggering. Some sources believe that the younger generation of people find it almost impossible to maintain focus for more than fifteen minutes at a time. This is incredibly detrimental to our ability to get tasks done and to make progress.

To that end I now recommend that you pick four random days within a two-week period where you record your hourly activities. Please use the days that are the most representative of your true day-to-day behavior if you want the best outcome from this evaluation.

Take special notice of the time you spend on your devices, this includes social media, emails, video, and surfing the web. Few people truly grasp the amount of time they spend being distracted throughout the day.

I also recommend that you take note of your sleep timing and quality during these days. Sleep is an integral part of overall health and sound judgment. If there is an area where you should try never to interrupt, it is a well-defined sleep schedule.

After you have completed your evaluation, there is usually no doubt that you have found some extra time that you can devote to your personal development, family, and business.

Use many different techniques to downregulate the use of these devices in your life. I love to ask people if they would ever take a job for free. One that would require their constant attention and would compare them with everyone else. Often these comparisons will end up making them lose focus on their own personal goals. This job will also require their attention at all hours of the day and night and keep them from making in-person connections with the people they love.

Most people look at me as if I have lost my mind, but the truth is that is what social media has become to most of society—a constant pressure to check in and to post.

Become the leader in your own life and take back control of your attention span and your expectations. I know that the genie is out of the bottle and social media is not going away. But as the leader, you can choose how it will be implemented in your life and organization. You can choose to turn off all notifications and to schedule a one-time-a-day check-in for no more than thirty minutes at a time. You can also choose not to post.

Learn that not everything needs to be posted and compared. This lesson will completely change the way you spend your days. Stop thinking that everything in your life needs to be posed, photographed, tweeted, and posted to make your life look amazing. This is an odd filter that we put on our personal life.

I see the effects this activity can have on families and children. Think about truly just being in the moment with your loved ones. No selfies. No smartphones on the dinner table. A vacation from Instagram. Take the time to look your friends and family members in the eye, make conversation, and engage with them regularly. Make the memories that last with them—no sharing required.

After some time of taking on this philosophy, you will become really surprised at the endemic nature of the devices we carry everywhere we go—in our hands, in our pockets and purses, mounted on dashboards, just an arm's length away. There are so many opportunities missed to actually communicate with people in person thanks to these impersonal technological "advances."

Just take the time to actually be in public without touching your phone. Strike up a conversation with someone, smile, and just enjoy meeting and greeting a real human in line at the grocery store, at the gas station, in yoga class, in the post office, while shopping or taking a walk or riding the bus or traveling. You will be surprised at the value that can be brought to your life through these opportunities, and the joy you can bring to others.

These in-person connections can bring a deep sense of contentment to your life. I have had some amazing conversations with kind people. I have received wonderful parenting encouragement from experienced grandmothers at the park. These interactions and opportunities for impromptu conversation and mentorship have brought me far more value than hanging out with Facebook during that time.

KEY INSIGHTS

- Perform a detailed personal SWOT analysis to develop a winning strategy.
- Perform a detailed time analysis to identify and mitigate distractions.
- Use social media as a tool and do not let it become your boss working you for long hours.

4

AVOID QUICKSAND—PLANT YOUR FEET ON THE ROCK

Define Yourself

Leadership is fraught with challenges from simple to complex. As a leader, you'll be faced with a never-ending supply of decisions that need to be made. There will be difficult conversations waiting to be had. Through all of this, knowing who you are is critically important. You need to develop a personal statement or philosophy. This statement is a truth about who you are and your personal purpose in life.

Many entrepreneurs and business owners are understandably highly motivated and excited at the launch of their businesses. They have spent so much time and energy planning the details. They are idealistically waiting for the pot of gold at the end of the rainbow. Even the most successful ventures have difficult challenges arise within the growth of their organizations.

How you meet these challenges will determine your strength as a leader. There is nothing better than knowing who you are when the rubber meets the road. Being excited and motivated is easy when situations are going well and you are successful. When times become difficult, however, having your personal statement to drive you forward will keep you strong and grounded as a leader.

To develop the personal statement, let's consider your best attributes. What makes you exceptional? This is a highly individualized process, so your personal statement should be unique to you. Are you a kind and creative person? Are you highly organized with massive internal strength? Take the time to write down your top attributes. Don't overthink. Just let the words flow with whatever comes to your mind.

If you are having difficulty with this task, ask a trusted friend or family member to work with you. Sometimes it can be difficult to see the really strong attributes that you have—especially if you have never looked internally before.

Once you have a page of attributes, let's talk about your personal purpose or philosophy in life. Are you interested in changing an area in someone's life? Do you wish to make the world beautiful through art? Maybe you want to help children.

Your personal purpose is your driver in life. This is something that is important to you on a level that you are willing to sacrifice for. A true purpose in life will keep you driven long after motivation fades. Emotional grit is founded in your personal statement and purpose.

Your personal purpose is not connected to your business; this is something that supersedes a business or organization. Develop a purpose outside of your business as part of the development of yourself as a leader. You should be more than just a job title. Who you are as a person should include the many aspects of your life.

This purpose may be what your business helps you to accomplish by giving you the resource of time or finances to complete. Have a personal purpose that is important in life. The joy and value that comes from having a purpose will strengthen your resolve and fill your life with contentment. Leaders worth following know who they are, especially when times get tough. They always recognize the value of working toward a purpose greater than themselves.

Now that you have your attributes and personal purpose written out, craft one or two sentences using this information. Keep it concise and simple—something that you will remember and can think of when situations get tough. This statement should be completely unique to you. In fact, it doesn't need to make sense to anyone but you. This is completely for your own personal use.

For example, my own personal statement is *Vikinger Exemplify*. These two words that have such deep meaning to me are not well understood by others. Nonetheless, over the past eight years this personal statement has pushed me to exceed my own expectations. When I have struggled with illness and thought I could not push through, these words gave me determination. I have fought through overwhelming and difficult times in life with this personal statement as a driving and never-ceasing force behind me.

If you realize the importance of this exercise and give it the attention it deserves, your personal statement will become at times a compass steering you toward land. Other times it will give you strength when you thought you had none left, and every day it should serve as inspiration to keep moving forward.

I have learned through time that if you do not define yourself and hold on to that through hard times, other people will seek to define you instead. Being defined by others is the antithesis of leadership.

Keep your personal statement somewhere where you see it every day. I keep mine written in the front of my journal. You could write it on a Post-it note and stick it to your bathroom mirror or fridge. Just place it where you will read it and be reminded of your strengths and determination daily.

Competition

Now that you have your personal statement prepared, the time has come to meet the true competition in your life. Go ahead. Stand in front of the mirror and say hello. That's right. The true and only competition for your life and leadership position is you. There is no other equally matched opponent than yourself. The work is in striving to improve yourself—that person in the mirror—every day. To work hard and show up for yourself even when it feels impossible or overwhelming.

Comparison runs rampant today thanks to the ever-increasing reach of social media. The constant fear of missing out can put leaders in awkward situations. Too often they make bad decisions trying to keep up with the fake facade they see reflected around them. This can be detrimental not only in your personal life but in your business life as well.

No one else on earth has the same strengths or challenges in life. No one has the same daily circumstances that you have. The idea that you can compare yourself to someone with a totally different life and expect some sort of true comparison is a misnomer. You are your perfect competitor. You alone have the exact same set of circumstances and attributes.

Start your day with the intent of working hard and improving yourself. Do not let others feel like competition; be happy for the success of others. Be grateful for the competitor in yourself and work to achieve your goals daily by showing gratitude for the wins and challenging opportunities that you face.

Life is about choices, and in this day and age many options are available. The truth is that no one can do it all. When you say yes to something, you are inevitably saying no to something else. The fear of missing out in that comparison race can cause you to lose focus and overextend yourself. When you lose focus on meeting your vision, you often find that you are unable to achieve the life you want; therefore, you end up not enjoying anything.

Take the time to consider yourself as a true competitor. Consider the areas in your personal life that are going really well and that you are excited about. Then take the time to consider areas of your life that you wish were going better.

Strive to improve your performance and resolve with each passing day. Align your daily habits with your vision and give it your all. When you get in the habit of pushing hard to meet your goals, you succeed. By performing your daily activities with precision and perseverance, you will begin to see marked change within your life. Something deep transforms when you begin to focus within and demand the most of yourself each day.

Shine the light of focus onto yourself and dim the light on others. You have incredible capabilities within yourself. When you decide and make the steps toward your goals, appreciable achievement will happen for you. You will no longer feel that fear of missing out and comparison in those that you see. Your light will shine bright, and you will push harder for yourself as the competitor daily.

Code for Life

Do you have a code that you live by? Many people find themselves susceptible to the peer pressure and persuasion of others because they lack a defined code for life. My grandfather used to always remind us that if we didn't stand for something, we would fall for anything. My grandparents were refined and principled people. As our culture and households have changed, this tenet seems to have gotten lost in the shuffle, and these principles seem to not be as readily defined in our lives.

The idea that as a leader we can just hold a focus group and tell you what people like is the downfall of true leadership. Strong leaders do not require a focus group to make decisions, nor do they attempt to please everyone. I am not talking about focus grouping whether or not someone likes chocolate or vanilla. I am talking about the decisions that are based on your moral and ethical beliefs.

Know what you stand for and what is in alignment with your personal statement and code for life because this will keep you making sound, consistent decisions for your life and your business. There will need to be decisions made every day for the welfare of your business. These decisions may impact many people from customers to employees.

Leaders have to make and be responsible for the "hard calls." If you live by a code, you know your values and the principles that you stand for. You would sacrifice and maintain strict discipline to follow the code you set for yourself.

Maybe you believe in the golden rule "Do unto others as you would have them do unto you." Maybe you follow the ten commandments or other religious affiliation.

Here is an example of the code that the Vikings lived by as seen in the *Havamal* in case you are of the warrior mindset:

Courage
Truth
Honor
Fidelity

Discipline

Hospitality

Industriousness

Self-reliance

Perseverance

Take the time to write out your code for life. Think through what you stand for and what you would be willing to defend and make sacrifices for. In leadership, you will be faced with making decisions that will not please everyone. Have a strong code that you live by that will inspire and give confidence to those around you.

Leadership that is consistent and true to maintaining integrity inspires loyalty in those who follow you and in your customer base. People will respect leaders that they see being consistent and not changing direction every time the wind blows.

You will build confidence in your decisions and be willing to defend them when you have a strong personal foundation. You will never please everyone, as you know, and the more that you try will degrade your foundation if you make concessions that do not align with your code for life. Have a clear code for life that you believe in which will give you the resolve and conviction to stand up when the situation requires you to be strong.

Vision

Entrepreneurship, business ownership, and leadership within an existing framework is on the rise. The age of technology and the internet have opened so many doors for individuals to take the opportunity to make something of their own. This is amazing and exciting. I love to see people reaching out and taking the leap.

As exciting as this news is, a dark undertone can often accompany these risks. Many new leaders find themselves underwater, overwhelmed, and faced with an unsustainable workload.

All too often a trail of broken dreams and families is left in the wake of the dream of business ownership. This is why I believe that having a well-thought-out vision is an essential part of leadership. You need to know what your priorities are and plan accordingly. You must focus and make decisions in alignment with your vision if you want to win in your personal and professional life.

You would never set sail on an ocean adventure without setting a trajectory and plotting a course. Why would you expect that in life you will end up where you want to be if you are not correcting course every time the wind changes or there are rough seas? Having a defined trajectory will inform all of the decisions that you make. Where you set your focus will determine where you end up in the long run.

Let's not leave our lives to chance. Let's take personal responsibility for setting the course and making the corrections as they become available.

What do you want in your personal life? Do you have a family already? Do you want a family in the future? What is important to you? Do you want to travel? Maybe you enjoy sports or other outdoor activities. Really take the time to think about what's on your bucket list.

If you have a family or spouse, I encourage you to work together on this vision. Make sure to include all the members of your family. When times get tough, you can all lean in toward your shared vision. You can make sure that your time together as a family is built on quality by forming a closer bond.

Dream big. This is your chance to imagine the possibilities that you want to incorporate into the story of your life. This world is full of many amazing opportunities and beautiful monuments all around the globe to see. Gorgeous mountains and ice blue oceans. The possibilities for your life are boundless when you set your vision.

If you are dreaming with your family, dream big together. I love to hear my son's ideas of becoming a scientist. How my husband wants to take the boys to places that are special to him and ride dirt bikes. For me I am always dreaming about hitting the open road in our motor home. I want to set off to find adventure and see all the national parks.

Although our lives have hit some bumps in the road, these dreams hold us together and allow us to lean in. So many can be pulled apart when life gets challenging, but a shared dream and goal can inspire teamwork and love in the most difficult of circumstances.

With your work vision, consider what will make you feel successful. What will let you feel that you have met your goal? Take the time to consider your ability to help others. The ability to grow your business. Maybe you have a specific financial goal. How do you feel when you visualize meeting this mark?

If you are having a hard time trying to build your vision, don't despair. This can be tremendously difficult if you have never taken the time to consider what you want out of your life. In the short term, consider some of the people in your life who are your role models. Think about what draws you to those people. Now think about some of the experiences you want in your life. As you practice and look inside yourself to what you are drawn to, your vision will become clear.

Nothing can be more devastating then entrepreneurs and leaders who finally "make it" in business only to find that they are incredibly unhappy. They realize that they sacrificed the relationships and experiences in life that would have brought them contentment and happiness, thinking they would get to the family stuff after they achieved professional success.

Now that your vision is clear in your mind, think about how the person you want to become feels. Maybe you feel happy, loved, powerful. Take the time to consider the person you want to become—how you feel and how you act.

Create a vision for your life and find your true north. Your vision is your direction for your life and includes all aspects of your personal and professional life. Your vision will allow you to become focused and to feel the sense of achievement as your life begins to match your vision. Know where you want to go and align your daily life actions with the vision that decreases fear of missing out.

Your vision will expand and contract throughout the seasons of your life. As you become the person your vision portrays, you will add to the picture for your life. You can use many different techniques to create your vision. You could make a vision board, a written list, a sketched picture, or a mental visualization. You should choose the type of vision that you are drawn to that feels the most real and tangible.

In addition, you should connect true emotions and feelings about how important achieving your vision is. Take time every day to think about your vision. This can be powerful in helping you to connect with achieving your vision especially as you face challenges in life.

Every day you will have the opportunity to become the person in your vision. People do not just wake up one day and become the person in their vision without a deliberate effort to do so. Now that you know the person you want to become, you will have the choice of becoming that person more and more every day. Take the time to be deliberate in your actions every day.

There is nothing more amazing than to see how setting a trajectory for your life and recognizing the type of person that you want to be can have a significant impact on your behavior. Align your daily actions with your vision, which will allow you to have optimal success within your life—although you will still face many challenges, and the path you take to meet your vision may change. If you know where you want to end up, you will give yourself a significant advantage in life. This vision will allow you to focus on the truly essential aspects that you need to feel happy and content.

Vision of Consequence

Today's society is fraught with distractions. There is a never-ending availability of time wasters at our fingertips and everywhere we go. Leaders must make deliberate choices with time management and focus if we want to accomplish our vision in life.

When situations arise where you find yourself having a difficult time staying disciplined and avoiding distractions, having a negative vision is an effective tool. A vision of what your life will be if you fail to stay disciplined in aligning your daily actions to your goals. You can use this vision of consequence to ask yourself if the hour of video games or social media is worth it. Will the lack of progress that may become your life if you do not remain disciplined be worth the reward of wasting time? Far too often in life we think it's just an hour of social media or video games.

Unfortunately, when we evaluate our time management, and if we are not meeting our goals, we will usually see that a large portion of our time is distracted. Our ability to maintain concentration has been hijacked by technology. Use your negative vision wisely with a true account of your time and efforts whenever you are having difficulty staying the course.

Everyone thinks that just having a positive vision is enough to keep you on track. I believe that the vision of consequence for your behavior can be an effective tool to keep meeting your true competitor daily. Definite consequences exist for every decision that you make in life. Although the occasional drift from your schedule may not be that big of a deal, certainly a routine distraction can derail your goals. A vastly real reminder of what the consequence will be for those distractions is important to have to keep you moving forward in a world that is filled with distraction.

Don't be afraid to use this tool when you find yourself drifting off course. Let your emotions really feel the pain of what it will mean to you for this to be your life reality. Determine whether whatever is pulling you away from being disciplined and completing your task is really worth the consequence. Don't wake up a year later to find yourself standing still and trying to figure out where all of the precious time of that year went.

KEY INSIGHTS

- Define yourself with a personal mission statement so others do not have the opportunity to do it for you.

- Meet the competition in the mirror and avoid comparison to others.

- Create a vison for your life and use it as a trajectory to guide you for your future success.

- Create the vision of consequence to remind you to avoid distractions that may keep you from reaching your goals.

5

MAKE IT HAPPEN THROUGH ACTION

Take Action

Now that you have written your personal statement, code for life, and developed your personal vision, you can create your action plan. The hardest task is sometimes the smallest. Often the distraction of what may happen or the need to organize and plan can detour you from the most important step.

Just begin—because your success for tomorrow or next year starts today. Allowing yourself to be distracted or overwhelmed may derail your opportunity. You could awaken five years from now and be no closer to your goals.

To begin is at times a most important action step to find success. Remember the first step is only that, an action. The action will not dictate the entire journey, nor will it guarantee success. There is a possibility of failure if you take the first step, but I guarantee you will fail if you don't take a step.

Take the time to break down each goal or vision you have into the required steps to complete. Then take those steps and actually schedule the activities into your calendar and take action. Daily completion and discipline will allow you to complete the required action steps to meet your goals. Once you begin to have wins, this process will become more detailed and easier to do.

Challenge yourself and commit to take your first step today even if it is the smallest step. Gain momentum through action.

Everyone has their own personal style of planning that seems to work for them. If you are already an excellent planner and are highly effective at executing and evaluating, then you may choose to stick with what works well for your own life.

Here I will give you an idea of the type of planning that I find highly effective. When developing my action plan, I have a short-term plan that is my yearly plan, which includes the year broken down into ninety-day blocks. I also have a three-year plan and a five-year-and-beyond trajectory.

Anything worth doing is worth doing well. This mindset will help to make sure that you are not taking on too many responsibilities when developing your plan. If you find yourself feeling rushed and just getting through tasks without doing them well, then you know you have taken on too much. When you find yourself in this situation, begin saying no to upcoming projects or opportunities or delegate some of the responsibilities to your support staff. You do not want to display yourself as a leader who is haphazard and does not do an excellent job. You do not want that to be your reputation with others that you may interact with in your personal and professional life. Becoming overextended can be a huge red flag for yourself as a leader.

Vision to Goal

Once you have your trajectory and vision well defined, it is time to break these down into goals. One system for writing goals is referred to as SMART goals developed by George T. Doran. This system can help you to develop time-oriented and metric-based goals. Let's go through the components of the SMART goals to get you started.

SPECIFIC	Your goal should be specific and well stated to what you plan to achieve.
MEASUREABLE	What are the metrics that you use to show that you are making progress or that you have met your goal?
ACHIEVABLE	Why is this achievable? What skills do you have that you will use to meet your goal?
RELEVANT	What makes this goal worth going after, and how is it relevant to helping you achieve your vision?
TIME-BOUND	What will the timetable be for meeting your goal? This should be realistic and specific.

Now that you have well-defined goals, determine what goal you will work toward first. You may feel that you need to do everything all at once. I caution against going gung ho all at one time. Remember that anything worth doing is worth doing well. You want to take on only what you can do with the mindset of excellence.

Take your top SMART goals and individually plot out all of the tasks it will take to complete the goal. This is an immensely important step to adding these goals into your action plan. Make sure that you give each step your best assessment of the time that will be needed to complete each task.

Frequently this part can be the breakdown point from goal to success. It can be easy to spell out your goals but actually segmenting them into actionable steps is necessary. Having a goal is not going to get you where you want to go unless you align your daily tasks to meet the goal. This step is critical to the success of your goals and vision.

Sometimes people think, well, those are small tasks, so do I really need to break them down and put them on the calendar? Do you want to succeed in the goal? If the answer is yes, then even the tiniest of all tasks needs to be defined and actually scheduled on the calendar. Be disciplined with yourself in this area.

Now that you have all of these steps listed by task, you can add them into your action plan. Make sure that you also schedule in your metrics at the appropriate time to evaluate.

Alignment

Leaders who want to be successful understand that you must align your daily actions with your vision to have success. Saying I want to lose weight is not enough; you must choose to stop eating dessert from the couch. If you want to meet your goal and have success, then you must work toward it through action daily.

For instance, the typical person eats approximately 1,095 meals per year and anywhere from 365 to 730 snacks. If you want to be successful in losing and maintaining your weight loss, then focus on meal prep is essential. If you plan and execute 1,000 meals and 600 healthy snacks in the year, then you will have aligned your daily eating habits with your vision.

In our modern world, adopting society's preprogramed autopilot is easy. We can quickly become overwhelmed and busy, so making concessions on what we perceive as little items can derail some of our most important goals. Stay focused on these tasks that are required to meet your vision, which is critical to meet your goals.

The truth is that our lives are made up of all the little choices and repetitive actions that we take every day. There may be a few truly large events that happen in your life, but the rest is the sum of all the little repetitive actions that add up to the measure of who you are. Recognizing that the little tasks can be so important is a total game changer. This mindset shift allows you to make the changes that will bring you the greatest contentment and joy in your life.

Short-Term Action Plan

The year segmented into four blocks allows you to be detail oriented and focused on actionable steps that can be taken in each ninety-day framework. Anything that is in my vision or required to accomplish my goals gets broken down into tasks required for completion and added to my ninety-day blocks. Have your goals outlined and scheduled into tasks; then you'll make meaningful progress toward the completion of your goals in easy day-to-day tasks.

At the end of the ninety days, I always complete a self-evaluation of the tasks that were done and reevaluate any items that were incomplete or not completed to my satisfaction. I then have the opportunity of completing those tasks in the next ninety-day block.

Year-End Review

After you have completed your four ninety-day blocks and the end of the year is coming to a close, the time has come to review the year that you have had before starting the new year. Our lives are so full with the to-dos of life that we often just drudge on not realizing how far we have come in a year.

Take a moment to consider how far you have come in your life in such a short amount of time. Think about the challenges that you have faced and how they have made you stronger or changed your mindset. Then celebrate the year and show gratitude for all you have faced. Whether you met all of your goals or had a tough year, celebrate. On the years that you totally hammer it home by meeting all of your goals, celebrate it just the same.

This is not about spending a bunch of money and taking a cruise around the world, although that does sound fun. This is about being grateful for all that the year brought you—even the challenges.

If any advice remained with me from some of my elderly patients when I was a paramedic, it was to enjoy the journey of life because it will be gone before you know it. In my younger years I dismissed this advice, as life seemed to be slowly moving by. It seemed as if it was taking forever to achieve my goals.

As I have gotten older and have children of my own, I realize just how important this advice truly is. Life seems to be flying by. Years are measured now in little marks on the wall as my boys grow taller. Life now seems to be moving at the speed of light, so this year-end review is a way to honor the journey to cement some of these experiences and challenges in our memories before moving forward.

Remember the challenges and the wins. The challenges are what make the wins amazing, and they transform and allow us to define ourselves. So make it a ritual to cherish the year that has passed before the new one begins and celebrate all you have achieved and overcome.

Three-Year Intermediate Plan

The three-year plan includes any of your longer-term goals that will take longer than one year to complete. For instance, maybe you have a financial goal or you are completing your degree. Action steps for these goals are included in the ninety-day blocking and beyond and include metrics and evaluation as well.

This is an excellent system for staying on track with longer-term goals that can easily be lost or put off due to events that seem more time sensitive.

Five-Year Trajectory

This is the area where you should make lifelong plans and long-term goal achievement. This is the area where your retirement plans and family trips that you plan to take when your children are older go. These are also plotted, and action steps that are required are collated in the ninety-day blocks to make these goals a reality in your future.

With any action plan that you develop, tasks and deadlines must be clearly defined and broken down in a way that you are able to complete them to the best of your ability. In addition to the tasks, I include all deadlines on the calendar. The final step is the evaluation of the task that will give you information about how you need to make adjustments in the future.

Remember that all leaders face challenges, and you may need to reroute plans and regroup to meet your goals. The fact that you have a detailed plan and metrics will help you to make changes to a plan should a challenge arise. This is not a free pass if you miss a goal due to lack of discipline or distraction. This is a recognition that there will be times in life when you may meet your goal by a different path.

Reevaluate your SWOT analysis at the end of your ninety-day block. Remember this is a perfect time to reevaluate your strengths, weaknesses, opportunities, and threats. As plans change, you can add them to your new ninety-day block.

Using your SWOT analysis can also help you identify threats to not meeting your goals. Once you have identified threats, use strategic planning to find ways to overcome these threats. Challenges may always pop up as you go. If you have identified something that may work against you in achieving your goal, make a plan to overcome that immediately. Leaders take the initiative to overcome adversity through strategic planning and implementation.

Any time you identify a threat to the success of your vision, goals, or business, define a strategy for overcoming it. Brainstorm and be creative because there is usually always a work-around or way to mitigate a threat, especially when you identify threats early on.

Let's take something simple: Clients who come to your office are routinely getting parking tickets in front of your building as a result of one-hour parking at the curbside. You could overcome this problem by identifying all of the parking structures or longer street parking in the three-block radius of your building. You could inform clients of available parking options in advance with a detailed email of the options with a map and cost of the parking. You could warn them in advance that the parking in front of your building is not favorable due to the short meter. In this way your clients can be informed and have all the information that is needed to mitigate this threat.

These types of early strategic planning to overcome threats can easily mitigate the negative impact that they can have on you and your clients. This simple work-around will make your customers feel informed and valued. You will avoid any negative impact that would result in unhappy clients leaving your building. Viola! A win-win for everyone with a simple strategy.

Evaluating Future Commitments

Are we as leaders too quick to say yes and overextend ourselves? There seems to be this possibility in many situations including networking events or PTA meetings. Although we may have the best intentions at heart, this demanding and fast-paced world can easily lead to becoming overleveraged.

I propose that we should be aware of our commitments for time, energy, and finances to determine what resources we have available. One technique is to accept opportunities that match well to your skill set and resources. For instance, if you are asked to bake cookies for a fund-raiser, and you haven't turned on the oven in ten years, this may be a stressful and difficult task. On the other hand, if the event organizers ask you to make some business calls and get some donations, this could tap into a top skill of yours and may only take a quick thirty minutes of your time. Consider how you can use the skills that will be helpful and also align with your particular set of resources.

The simple art of accepting opportunities that align with your skill set can allow you to contribute to the community without becoming a burden. Only accept requests for help that you can comfortably manage, which will allow you to engage happily and be excited for the next opportunity to be involved.

KEY INSIGHTS

- Build momentum for success by taking action.
- Break your vision into SMART goals that can be put into action.
- Develop action steps from your SMART goals and schedule them into your calendar to achieve them.
- Create your ninety-day, three-year, and five-year plans to keep you on track.
- Celebrate the success and challenges that you have had every year.

6

AVOID THE CRASH— PREPROGRAM YOUR AUTOPILOT NOW

Time—A Finite Resource

Everyone is given exactly twenty-four hours in a day. Time is a truly finite resource in life.

Although no one can predict the number of days they will be given in their lives, how you use your time will impact your ability to live your vision and to have success within your business.

Now that you have examined your time through evaluation, this is an excellent opportunity to determine your true priorities in life. What is truly important to you to accomplish with the time you have? If you learn to cut the distractions and focus on your top priorities in life, you will gain a sense of accomplishment.

Develop the primacy mindset, which will be an impactful tool to maintain your focus on the most important priority for you in your life. Try to remove items and responsibilities from your life that are not in alignment with your vision. Items or activities that require your time, effort, and energy are not your top priority, and they can serve to derail your progress by splitting your focus.

I have heard many successful leaders in life talk about how they focus on only one priority at a time. Although they may have many tasks that they want to accomplish in life, they only think of one at a time. After giving their full attention to that single priority and completing it, they move on to the next priority on their list.

I too incorporate this in my life. I keep one family priority and one professional priority. These are the areas where I keep my main focus for moving forward. This primacy mindset allows you to become incredibly effective in completing the tasks that you focus on.

Here are a few of the strategies that I have incorporated in my own life that help to keep me in alignment with my primacy mindset. We can manage many areas in life effectively by putting in systems that work to decrease our overall time commitment. Having these systems has also decreased my stress level and allowed me to have more energy to spend with my family.

Minimalism

People adopt strategies to help them have more time in each day for the important events that matter. In fact, an entire movement has been created around the idea of minimalism—a concept that encourages getting rid of items so that you can free your time and space from clutter and duty to the items. This is a thought-provoking concept for many people.

The idea is that maybe we have all been marketed to on such a level that we have bought into material items instead of connection with others in a search for contentment. The thought is that having the newest, shiniest everything will somehow fill the void of discontentment. The marketing that has been unleashed on our society is based in the human emotional element that provokes a sense that items will bring happiness. Usually this happiness is short-lived, and then we look for the next item that will fill us with joy, even if only for a moment.

Different schools of thought are available for this concept of minimalism. Some people feel that stark white with one outfit and a few dishes is best. Others feel that you can have a specific number of items as long as they all serve multiple purposes within your day. I believe that the diminishing of emotional connections to items and an elevation of your priorities and experiential adventures is an ideal goal. I believe that clearing the clutter and having a well-organized home that fills you with a sense of pride and comfort is a perfect foundation. The application of minimalism is different for each individual and family.

Marie Kondo, an organizer and author of a popular book and movement on the topic, the Kondo method, has developed a plan for decluttering your whole home. In her method she has you work in a specific order gathering all the items from that particular subset. She then encourages you to hold the items and keep only the items that spark joy. After you have discarded additional items through donation, sales, or garbage, you can move on to organization. Her specific folding method and organizing plan helps to keep everything in drawers and visible for use.

I personally quite enjoyed her book and her method while downsizing for our cross-country adventure. I found it easy to use with my whole family, and the mindset shift it gave us increased our gratitude for the experiences and items that did bring us joy. The idea that our other items would then be set free to bring joy to others was especially useful when working with my young son. He was happy to send his toys on for their new lives in new homes. I highly recommend her book (*The Life-Changing Magic of Tidying Up*) to anyone who is looking to make such a change.

My family had a wonderful experience of downsizing into a fifth wheel for a year and a half. The need to pack up and move cross-country gave us an opportunity to check out different states. We made sure that we liked our new city before putting down more permanent roots.

My husband and young son were initially hard pressed to downsize to that level. As the process continued, we quickly realized that the items in life held little value. We were surprised to find the time that we gained not having to care for all those extra items was invaluable.

For myself, going through Kondo's method helped me to make a complete mindset shift from quantity to quality. As I went through my home, choosing what to keep for our adventure, the items that sparked joy were surprising. I tended to feel amazing thinking of all of my best items that I barely ever used that I only brought out for special occasions.

Because I needed to really cut the number of items that I had, I was forced to make a choice. Either I would let go of the belongings that truly sparked joy for me, or I would use my best every day. As I thought about this, I began to wonder what was a special day. What was I waiting for to use these items such as dishes and clothes that I loved so much that rarely saw the light of day?

I leaped forward with these items that I loved and got rid of all the other "stuff" that I no longer needed. I now use my best every day. Doing this really changed the way I think about my belongings. I want every day to actually be my best. I wear clothes that make me feel feminine and beautiful. I have only a few items, so I choose clothing of quality and put them to use.

My family routinely eats dinner on gorgeous china that I inherited from my grandparents. This beautiful china set that my grandparents received for their wedding is now about seventy years old. The beautiful white china with a silver rim brings a smile to my face. I remember lovely moments with my grandmother in her kitchen. I can think back to her serving me my meals on that same china when I was six. I think I was the only one who ever even ate on that china, but for some reason I loved it.

My grandmother had a way about her. She was comforting and kind and always made us feel like we were worth her best. I now hope that I am leading through example to my own children in this way. Enjoy your best every day and be your best every day. What are you waiting for?

When you think out of the box on some of these social norms, it will open many doors for you. Take the opportunity to consider how downsizing in your life can free you to have new experiences. Whether or not you are ready to pare down all your belongings or just make some slight changes, there is an opportunity for growth in this experience itself. There is also the opportunity that items you no longer need or use could be used by others when you donate them.

When determining if you need to clear clutter or change your home, consider the cost of time and attention that you spend minding the items in your life. Let this be your guide in making changes to your home and life.

Capsule Wardrobe

I personally love the idea of a capsule wardrobe and have been practicing it for many years. In my former life I wore a uniform to work for seventeen years. This was so simple and stress-free and allowed me to have a small wardrobe for days off. As I continued my career outside of EMS, having a simple professional uniform—just a couple of outfits—makes mornings care-free and easy.

Having a small wardrobe of items that fit you well and make you feel confident is extremely freeing. Although you may think this way of dressing is restrictive, I never feel that way. I pay close attention to the items that I buy so that I feel my best in each of them, which makes it so easy to get dressed in the morning feeling confident in my choice of outfit.

Shopping for quality and fit is now a priority. I no longer pick items that are trendy for the season, and that helps decrease decision fatigue. With practice this curated wardrobe will take on a distinct personal style unique to you. This strategy is amazing for men and women alike. You can also apply it to children so you can cut down on the morning routine shenanigans.

I personally follow the ten-item wardrobe system by Jennifer L. Scott. Scott is a *New York Times* best-selling author for her Madame Chic series (*Lessons from Madame Chic*). The Daily Connoisseur YouTube channel that she runs has helpful information about developing and maintaining your curated wardrobe. This system makes it so simple to build a workable wardrobe that you love.

Her practical system helps you to define your sense of style and love the clothes that you have. Scott helps you shift through the seasons by purchasing only what you need to complete your wardrobe after an item has been removed. I love the confidence that she has developed by looking presentable every day and knowing that no one cares if what you're wearing is part of a small, defined wardrobe.

Although her books and channel are geared toward the feminine audience, her system is easy to apply to men as well. I have helped my husband develop a simple wardrobe that he loves. My children also love their wardrobes that have been made using the same principles.

I did expand the number of pieces for the boys as they are never afraid to get dirty or tear a knee in their pants. These small selections save us so much time and energy. They all have their own sense of style that seems to match the individuality of all of our personalities. This plan is also a huge money saver since we only purchase what we need, and we wear our clothes frequently.

There are many other approaches to capsule wardrobes, so just pick one that you are drawn to and give it a try. If you have a larger budget, this is an area that you could consider outsourcing to a personal stylist. Many stylists now focus on developing small capsule wardrobes that have excellent fit and match the style that you are trying to develop.

If you want to look professional but you have a hard time choosing clothing that is flattering to your figure, a stylist can be an excellent professional to hire. Of course, you need to make sure that this service is in your budget and that you are buying clothing that you can actually afford should you choose to work with a professional.

Meal Planning

Meal planning and meal prep is a winning strategy for superior nutrition. Having recipes that are easy to make and include a lot of the same ingredients can save time and frustration in the kitchen. Meals are incredibly important considering eating is one of the most repetitive actions you will take throughout your lifetime. Food is fuel for your body and brain. Food is also information for your DNA and repair system. We need to get our food plan and preparation right.

I, for one, do not want to rely on food prepared outside my home for the majority of my meals. Preparing meals where I know the ingredients and quality is important to maintaining my health and that of my family. This does not need to be time-consuming or overwhelming. You can adopt one of many systems and schedules. I think simple is best. Research shows that people who adhere to a regimented and minimally varied food plan have the best health outcomes.

Find yourself a core meal plan of about seven to fourteen meals that are healthy and filling for you and your family. Now mix and match those throughout the week, making extras for lunches as a bonus. This simple plan can keep your health on track and keep you out of the drive-through or restaurants. If you have extra time, then make exotic recipes on one of your days off throughout the week to keep meals spicy.

In the event that you just really do not cook or you are not in a living situation where you have access to a kitchen, other options are available. Meal prep services can be delivered to your home or office. Through local food preparation services and grocery stores, you can pick up food for the week, and they cater to many differing dietary needs. Many of these food services also work with local food sources and have organic options.

Just know that having healthy food at the ready will have an impact on your overall sense of well-being and your emotional resilience. Do your homework and be prepared.

When life gets overwhelming and you feel as if you are struggling to just survive the rigors of life, you need to slow down. Often just taking the opportunity to evaluate the areas that are causing you so much stress can help you build in a system that allows you to accomplish the tasks with ease. Don't be afraid to slow down and regroup when life begins to outpace the number of hours in the day.

These strategies can all be applied to your life to allow you to simplify and elevate the people and experiences in your life that matter the most to you. These sometimes-drastic changes can open doors to get you out and see the world to enjoy the beauty of nature.

Outsourcing and Delegation

Now that you can see how important time is to you as the leader, learning to use resources appropriately becomes an imperative. I offer two resources that you can consider as the work around you begins to pile up: outsourcing and delegating.

Outsourcing is the act of hiring a professional or freelancer to complete a project or job that they are qualified to do. There is an important difference between delegation and outsourcing in that outsourcing is working with qualified professionals where you have recourse if a job is not done to your satisfaction. These resources will cost you money depending on the scope of work that you need and the level of experience of the professional.

You want to remain fiscally responsible when hiring, but I rarely hire anyone who just quotes me the lowest price. Look for professionals who have enough of a work history that you can clearly evaluate their level of work, and that you feel comfortable they will be able to perform required tasks to your level of expectation.

Delegation is using your in-house resources such as other employees or, for some at home, maybe a spouse or family member. Having the ability to delegate some tasks to your in-house staff and family is a helpful resource to use when appropriate.

When you are delegating, you are responsible for choosing the right person for the job. You are also responsible for the oversight of the task. This can be a less expensive route to go if the task is not highly technical and fits well into the skill set of your chosen partner for the task.

For example, you decide that you want a professional Adobe layout ebook that is interactive for your website done in-house. When you delegate it to an employee, you need to make sure they have the appropriate tools and know how to perform the task.

If you assign this technical project to an employee who lacks the skill set necessary to complete the project, you may have just wasted a complete week of pay to that employee who could have been completing other tasks, and you may still need to outsource that job to a professional. A professional with the appropriate skills might easily complete the task in a day for a cheaper price than what you pay your employee. When deciding whether or not to outsource or delegate, do a bit of fact finding and make sure you choose wisely the appropriate person for the task.

When you are going to delegate or outsource, you need to be clear and concise about exactly what you are expecting for your project. You should always use examples and pictures when possible to clearly explain your vision for any project.

In addition, your timeline should be clearly defined before the project begins. Make sure that whoever you use to complete projects for you has clear guidelines. They should know to immediately contact you should they require further information or have a problem completing your project in the way you requested. As the leader, being clear when assigning work can save you many headaches in the future.

Now that you can see the difference between the two resources that you can use for keeping your workload in check, make sure that you know your time and financial resources that you have at your disposal. These are two important considerations when determining what projects get outsourced versus delegated. The more that you can outsource specialized tasks, the more time and energy you have to put into other parts of your business.

Consider outsourcing jobs where mistakes can cost you big in the long run—for instance, accounting and legal work. Any time you have a risk for large fines or mishaps when you are not in compliance, you want to use an expert and outsource.

Hard Work vs. Working Smarter

Hard work is a tenet of success. I believe this to my core. If you want to be successful in life, you will need to be disciplined and put in the hard work. There will be times in life that you will definitely need to hustle and make some sacrifices. We as leaders need to determine the lengths of time that this is healthy in life.

The truth is that when we go long periods of time under chronic stress and not meeting our physiological needs for sleep and recovery, we have diminishing returns. Are we truly better off to burn the midnight oil? I think that as new leaders and business owners, we feel the need to do everything, so pushing ourselves can be detrimental to ourselves, our employees, and our businesses.

Chronic long-term stress has been highly linked to adverse health conditions and obesity. Determine how often you should burn the midnight oil for yourself and your employees. You should look into this deeper to decide if such effort is worth it. Is this for a one-time project that you are just completing? Will you be expected to perform at a high level the following day without the requisite rest and recovery time? What would be the point of pushing yourself in this way only to end up quite ill later in life? What if you are unable to enjoy the success you may amass? You also don't want employees who are consistently missing work due to illness or making bad judgment calls due to the consistent overuse.

Working smarter is the concept of doing blocks of intense, undistracted work where you are capable of completing large projects in smaller periods of time. This is the type of work that requires strategic planning and assigning work in a way that it can be completed in blocks. The use of resources in a strategic way is incredibly important when developing this type of strategic plan. When you are using employees, make sure that you assign projects based on skill set for the best outcome.

Push through when you must. There may be times when you have a tight deadline or increase in demand that requires all hands on deck. In these defined situations you want to make sure that the overload does not go on for more than a short period of time. Long hours and pushing through is completely unsustainable for everyone's health and well-being. When you push yourself and your employees longer than these periods of time, you risk decreased overall productivity, illness, absenteeism, and decreased morale.

I meet so many people who started out with this push-through mentality. They did not prioritize the need to take care of themselves. They would tell themselves that they would rest and do all of those tasks later. Later never came, and their lives became completely unsustainable. They are run down, working too much, and feeling as if they have no way to make changes.

Feeling completely trapped in a life where you are overwhelmed and have no joy or contentment is a sad result of not aligning your vision to your daily life. Although your life may seem completely locked-in, this is rarely the case. With fresh eyes and a clearly defined trajectory, even the most entrenched people can find relief with clear and deliberate moves.

In this same arena, you as the leader should consider whether or not your place of employment will allow overtime on a regular basis. Employees who are working increased hours can become overwhelmed. The simple act of their taking on so many hours of work—and missing out on any happiness in their lives—can be truly detrimental to the morale of these employees.

If you are taking on tactics such as increased wages, profit sharing, or other incentives with your employees, this may be something that you choose to disallow for the health of your employees and work environment. By treating your employees as an integral part of your team, and compensating above the bare minimum, when profits allow, your employees can also pursue meaningful lives outside of work.

If you have a short-term project where you need some extra hours from employees, fine. If, on the other hand, you have an overflow of work on a regular basis, it will be time to consider taking on a new employee or maybe starting an intern position. This is an area where you should lead by example by loving your life outside of work.

Multitasking and Balance

The idea that you can multitask and have a balanced life tends to keep people from accomplishing work tasks to their best ability or finding contentment in their home life.

When you are working on a task, you need to give your full attention and focus to the problem at hand for an excellent result. Conversely, when spending time with family and friends, they deserve to have your undivided attention and concern. If you spend your entire time with your loved ones while answering emails or talking on the phone, clearly your time and attention is elsewhere. That is not balanced. These are the choices that we make in life. Where you put your focus is your priority, which is communicated through your actions.

These old ways of thinking can be reframed so that you are fully present in the moment and show up with a mindset of excellence in each situation. Think of balance as giving your all in each situation throughout your day. Schedule your day to include clear work hours that are uninterrupted and where you have deep, productive progress. When you are at home, turn off your notifications and put your phone away. Spend your time fully engaged with your loved ones. This communicates value and respect to those around you.

When you have dinner with friends, make it a point not to engage with your phone and ask them to do the same. Give yourself the opportunity to have genuine, respectful connection. Allow yourself to not have a fear of missing out in those moments, so just embrace the friendship and bonding that happens without the interruption of our devices.

I have a perspective of regret that was formed through my time as a paramedic. Having been with many people during tragedy and loss allowed me to see how regret can surface at the end of people's lives. Relationships and family can easily be put off until later, we think in that moment, believing that later will be just around the corner.

Unfortunately, this is not always the case. I never heard anyone with a serious medical emergency tell me that they wished they had spent more time climbing the corporate ladder or pushing harder at work. Usually the regrets were far more personal, having to do with opportunities missed with children and spouses.

With this in mind, I urge you as a leader to take time in your day to really focus on your vision and the top priorities that you have in your life. I believe that taking the time for your loved ones every day is truly important. Make your moments count even if your time is limited. Take the time to make moments and memories especially with your spouse and children.

You will never get those moments back. Your children will grow and your spouse will fill their time without you, while you spend every waking moment focusing on building your business and the hustle and bustle of entrepreneurship.

At the end of the day there is nothing better than having family and friends to share your success with.

A Winning Routine

I love all the attention that is given to morning routines these days. I believe that a defined morning and evening routine can be essential to success. Start your day with a plan; this is a winning strategy.

Unfortunately, copying the millionaire morning routine does not turn you into a millionaire. You will find that successful leaders definitely share some of the same morning and evening habits. Consistency is a key factor for success. Having a defined, consistent routine that helps you to feel prepared and cared for can go a long way in tackling your leadership role.

The repetitive nature of the morning routine can have a profound, calming effect as you start your day. I always caution people to use their morning to set a tone to their day. I recommend that no time or attention be given to email or social media. Do not let others influence the start of your day. Work in some time to have silent contemplation and set an intention for the day.

The truth is that we all lead incredibly different lives, and developing the winning routine is again highly specific to our own individual needs. My routine has changed drastically throughout the phases in my life especially with the addition of a husband and children. Your morning routine should include enough time for you to be ready and out the door, starting your day without being rushed and no unnecessary stress. Wake up early and give yourself personal time for reflection, exercise, and meal prep so you can really start your day off well.

Take the time to sit down and build out your ideal morning. Make sure that you start your day with a plan, know what your day looks like, and give yourself time to be physically and emotionally prepared for the rigors of your day.

If you have children, make sure that they also participate in the morning and evening routine as soon as they are old enough. I always make sure that my children have all of their clothes and school items ready to go so that mornings run smoothly and we have time for family breakfast in a calm way before the day begins. This bonding time as a family is amazing and fun. It helps me to feel focused during my busy hours knowing that my children have everything they need and had the opportunity to connect with me in a loving way.

Your evening routine is an excellent time to allow for contemplation and gratitude for the opportunities that you encountered throughout your day. Also make sure that you are including quality connection with your loved ones. Make sure to plan for an optimal amount of high-quality deep sleep.

Sleep is again essential for maintaining your emotional resilience and sound judgment as a leader.

Your day-off plans should include genuine rest and relaxation time for recovery from the week. Make sure to schedule time with family and friends to maintain the all-important social connection. On the day before you return to work, take a small amount of time to meal plan, grocery shop, and meal prep. This will start your week out for success.

Spontaneous. Who Me?

I love when people ask if leaders can ever just be spontaneous and make a decision on the spot. That somehow planning is inhibiting the ability to have some fun. Could they play hooky for the day?

Plan and know your resources, which allows for you to make spontaneous decisions in the moment while not having negative consequences. Leaders who build a life they love and take the time to build in resources by being deliberate have opportunities that others do not.

When you have extra money in the bank and all of your work is done and you get an invite to go somewhere spur of the moment, confidently accept. Go have fun. Be in the moment and make amazing memories.

When you are the leader who has mentored and trained trusted employees who can run the business, go on vacation. Go have fun knowing that your business is in the hands of those you trained and trust that they are loyal to you. When you take the time to train people well, you can be confident that they will be prepared to make decisions in your absence.

This discipline of planning and preparing opens so many doors in the future. As you build resources, you will have more opportunities to say yes. Know that when you initially stick to your discipline, you can efficiently build your business and resources through planning and execution to give you the best opportunities. Work hard, show up, put in the effort, and be deliberate so that you can have experiences that you earned in life later.

The freedom you can create for yourself is amazing when you make the initial sacrifice for success. Pay attention to the way you build your life and organization. Take on only what you can do with the mindset of excellence, and respect yourself and your family enough to say no when the situation dictates it. Stand firm when you need to so that you can enjoy all the freedoms this will create for your future.

KEY INSIGHTS

- Time is a finite resource in life; use it wisely and build a life you love.

- Minimalism can be an effective tool for clearing unnecessary items in your life.

- Capsule wardrobe is an opportunity to dress for success effortlessly every day.

- Meal planning can put your nutrition on the right track and keep you feeling amazing while you chase your dreams.

- Outsourcing and delegation are excellent resources to free up your time and attention for items that only you can accomplish.

- Work smarter not harder by recognizing that true balance comes when attention is given to one thing at a time.

- Separating work time from time with family and friends can lead to greater efficiency and contentment.

7

BOSS 101

Personal Responsibility

To be successful in a leadership position, you must develop a strong internal locus of control. Having a strong internal locus of control means that you believe that your actions and contributions will have an impact on the outcome of situations.

Leaders who accept that challenges that happen are just part of life and take initiative to overcome those challenges have the greatest opportunity for success. You may require additional support or resources, but you deliberately seek them out. You come up with a plan to overcome problems as soon as they are found. There is no room for a victim mentality or waiting for someone to come save you when you are the leader.

If you learn to think outside the box and to consistently look for the next best step, you can stay the course for your business. In many situations the original plan may need to be reworked, or a change will need to be implemented. Have a strong plan and execution but also be flexible in the process; then you can be strategic in the moment. This flexibility will allow you to avoid the pitfalls that can arise when leadership becomes too rigid in their thinking and actions.

You will face many constraints with your business, and you will be required to make choices. The constraint of time, money, employees, and resources can be excellent opportunities to innovate and be creative and take personal responsibility. Rethink the resources you have and come up with new and exciting answers to the problems.

I think of the Apollo 13 mission that never quite made it to the moon. Under the inspired leadership of Gene Kranz, mission commander at NASA, if it was not for his unwavering leadership and dedication to the concept that failure is not an option, Apollo 13 would have been doomed. Kranz had an excellent leadership perspective and mindset for excellence that he clearly demonstrated to his team even during crisis situations. He once said, "To recognize that the greatest error is not to have tried and failed, but that in trying, we did not give it our best effort."

Although there were many opportunities for failure and complete defeat on that doomed mission to the moon, he stood firm. Kranz believed in the ingenuity and excellence of his team. He directed them to not only face the challenges that they were presented but to overcome them. Under his leadership the department managers were able to delegate effectively.

"Apollo succeeded at critical moments like this because

the bosses had no hesitation about assigning crucial tasks to one individual, trusting his judgment, and then getting out of his way," Kranz said.

The NASA team had severe constraints when overcoming the dangers for the mission crew. They could only use what was available to the three astronauts in the Apollo 13 spacecraft. Despite all the odds and the obstacles they faced when an oxygen tank exploded, they were victorious in their mission to bring home the three American astronauts: Jim Lovell, Fred Haise, and Jack Swigert.

These brave men and women of mission control had the initiative to meet the challenge. They did believe in taking responsibility for their areas of expertise, and as a result a situation that could have been dire became victorious. Each member of the team had to be responsible for moving their area of expertise down the court. There was no time for excuses or rescue parties. There was no room for error in a mission that lasted only twelve days.

What could have been considered a failure of their initial plan to land on the moon became a proud moment for NASA in their ability to respond to a life-threatening crisis in space.

Take the ultimate responsibility for failure and recognize that the decisions and behaviors that you model for your team are of the utmost importance. That's how you gain the respect of others around you.

Train your mind to be detail-oriented and flexible and to always ask what is the next best step. The next best step may be a move that you have never considered. You may have to step completely out of the box to overcome the challenges. Know your resources and the strengths of your team, which will allow you to formulate a strategy to move forward.

Leaders who wait for help or for someone else to save them usually find themselves in the unemployment line.

Show up Like a Boss

When you are at work or in your daily life, show up like you mean business. Stop going through life with this chillax attitude like sweats are now your dress code for any event. Unless you are a fitness coach or an athlete, the sweats should stick to the gym or yoga class.

Dress like you mean business. Remember the old saying: look good, feel good, do good? This is a real axiom so take the time and effort to dress for success. This does not mean that you need to spend a fortune on clothes. It does mean that you need to make the effort to dress for success in your own style. How you dress communicates to others around you, so pay attention to the message you are sending as the leader.

Put thought into the message that you send through the way you dress and the words you use. These nonverbal and verbal communications can make critical impressions on people that you interact with on a daily basis.

Although I would tell you not to judge a book by its cover, in business sometimes all you see is the cover. There is steep competition in the professional market, and although you may have a lot to offer, you may lose out in the first round if you do not present yourself in an organized and professional way.

Show up on time or even early. Just because you are the boss and you can set your own schedule does not exempt you from being on time. When you set a meeting or start time, show up. This is another area where you are setting the example to others around you.

Show respect to the people that you have meetings with because their time is valuable, too, and they do not want to sit around waiting for you because you didn't plan your time appropriately. This lack of respect can really put a bad taste in people's mouths. Unless you had an unavoidable tragedy, make it a point to be on time.

Prepare in advance for meetings or presentations. You are the leader and are setting the tone for the others involved. Look over all materials and do any research that you need to in order to be well versed in any material that will be seen in a meeting. Not only do you not want to be the last one to know about the information, but you want to be able to evaluate suggestions and proposals with confidence. Being the leader is not a fly-by-the-seat-of-your-pants position.

Develop an eye for detail in any of the materials that you will be presenting for your business. Make sure that your website is functioning appropriately and that your handouts are grammatically correct. These simple areas where the public make contact with your business may be your only chance to impress them.

I personally do not want to do business with companies that do not take the time and energy to present me with well-formulated information. I'm far less worried about the flashiness of the website or the handout as I am the actual content. Do your homework and present information that is correct and relevant in your business genre.

Personal Development

Taking on the position of leadership is an exciting step in life. The leadership role can be one of personal satisfaction and freedom. You must never forget that this role demands significant care and responsibility. Anyone who wants to excel and grow in a leadership position must take care to develop themselves as a leader and human.

The weight of leadership can be all encompassing, and the best leaders know that, to carry the weight and respond with grace and resolve, they must be calm, capable, and content in their own personal life. How can a leader care about the happiness and success of their employees and customers if they feel completely run down and dissatisfied in their own life?

When your needs are not met as a person in your own day-to-day life, it can be difficult to encourage others to pursue happiness. Taking care to ensure that the foundations of health and happiness are met in your own life is of the utmost importance to your success as a leader.

A never-ending to-do list will require your attention. Learn to be highly deliberate and surround yourself with people you can trust and delegate work to. This is an important foundation. This foundation will allow you time to focus on your vision and work toward daily personal development. Some of the areas that can be the most rewarding are the connections you have with your family and friends, hobbies, activities, personal health goals, and quiet contemplation.

There is usually a push in business to constantly focus on your work—to be driven at all hours of the day or night. I caution against this for leaders and employees. The attention that you give to your personal development will be so valuable to you and your business. The small amount of time that you dedicate to improve yourself outside the business will increase your ability to lead and innovate within the business. Working hard daily is imperative to business success, but I would argue that time devoted to your personal well-being and development is just as critical. This time and effort will keep your batteries charged and keep the leadership role sustainable over the long haul.

The Mindset of Excellence

Develop a mindset of excellence, which is a valuable skill for a leader. This is not to be confused with the concept of perfectionism. Perfectionism is a focus on the outcome of an action; whereas, excellence is a mindset that focuses on the effort.

The development of the mindset of excellence will serve you in any stage of life. Whether you are working for someone else or for yourself, you should think of any task as something you will do to the best of your ability.

The work you put in is always a reflection of you and no one else. Learn to show up for yourself and put the effort into anything you do that will change you. You will develop a respect for the effort that is required to do tasks well.

Remember that life is made up of all the small tasks and details that make up the days and years of your life. If you want to be ready to perform with the mindset of excellence in some large important task, it starts with the training of the small tasks.

Think of the mindset of excellence as if you were an athlete who practices every day for the Olympics. When you arrive at the competition, it's just another day of practice. Not only will you become more skilled in the actions that you do by putting in the effort, but you will find that the discipline of this mindset will pay off big when you are leading others. Recognize that leading by example with a mindset of excellence is how to prepare for success for yourself and those around you.

I challenge you to put this into practice today. Start showing up for yourself and know that you are responsible for the outcome of your own effort. You will find that, after you develop this practice fully in your own life, the saying about the way you do something is the way you do everything takes on a whole new meaning. You will begin to see that the people who chillax their way through life are not the people that you will look to when you are expecting a job to be done with excellence.

The mindset of excellence can become highly visible to you daily when you start putting this technique into practice in your own life.

Have you ever gone somewhere to grab your morning cup of coffee and been greeted with a smile? The professional behind the counter takes their time to give you undivided attention while commenting politely to you with pleasant small talk. Your coffee is made with excellence to your order specifications. As you sit to enjoy the coffee, you watch the coffee professional greet the regulars, every single one by name. No need for them to even give her the order as the barista knows them all by face.

The coffee professional continues about the day's work carefully, taking care to do the tasks while smiling and checking in on the customers. This level of excellence with a pleasant attitude can completely change the way your day starts. Now that is the person I would want to hire every day of the week.

The Art of Mentorship

The privilege of mentorship to the next generation is a tradition that is rooted in human history. The experienced people teach and prepare the young to move forward and take their place in society. This somewhat lost art in today's culture is rewarding in ways that cannot be explained. I often think of those that came before us. How would they teach their craft or life's work to the next generation? So much wisdom was communicated to our ancestors in this way.

There seems to be an ever-changing thought that you can become an expert in anything by watching a few YouTube videos—always looking for a hack or way to be an expert without the requisite time and effort that would earn you that title.

Although you can learn many skills from the internet, the human face-to-face connection and taking-under-the-wing mentoring is different. This should be a special honor to learn and be fostered by an established leader. Building a genuine respect for the discipline and daily challenges of the mentor allows for a respect for the older generation.

The respect that is established allows for the new generation to understand the ways in which things have been done while also learning to innovate for the benefit of all. The balance that is created between the old and new helps to define a common goal for the future.

Once you have firmly planted your feet in your leadership position and have had time to gain knowledge and wisdom, take on the role of mentor. Wisely choose individuals in whom you recognize a foundation of respect and coachability. Share your wisdom and knowledge and the nuance of the leadership role that you have learned. Rejoice with your prodigy in their success and opportunities as they grow into their leadership role. There is no need to take on every bright employee that you have contact with to attempt to share your wisdom.

Giving back is rewarding on so many levels. This simple taking back of tradition and seeking out excellence in lifelong learning—a dedication to improving yourself—will only be enhanced while teaching the new generation of leaders. You will be challenged to continue learning and stretching yourself as you educate.

I am grateful for the leadership that mentored me. The opportunities that I had to learn from such skilled providers and leaders and the confidence that I gained and the doors such mentoring allowed me to step through were remarkable. I have the utmost respect for those who forged the way for women as paramedics. These men and women taught me more than I could ever have learned through a book. They were willing to give back to the young who would continue where they left off.

As a paramedic, I appreciated my role as both preceptor and field training officer. It was rewarding to give back to the paramedics who would take up the charge when I had moved on. Taking on the tradition of teaching leadership, medicine, and the art of compassion enriched my life on so many levels. I rejoice in the success of all my students as they have gone on to make amazing careers. I know that if my family is ever in need that they are dedicated caregivers and are compassionate to the human suffering that they see. This has led to a substantial feeling of accomplishment in my life.

The leaders you train are not your competition. So many business owners and leaders express concern that if they give away their secrets to success that these young entrepreneurs will use it to put them out of business. Although this could be true, it has not been my experience. When you take on a student of strong moral character and respect, they look to you with genuine gratitude. You may just find them to be someone to take on the torch of your business when you are ready to leave or be a strategic business partner in the future. If you're lucky, the student will at some time surpass the mentor, assuring that progress in the next generation will be worth paying attention to.

I believe that the passing on of information in this personal mentorship approach is an important tradition that should be continued. This is not just about reading a mentee a leadership book or teaching them techniques they could learn from school. This is about leading by example and helping to foster opportunities for growth, and opening doors that may otherwise have been impossible for them to go through. This type of personal caring for the next generation is an important way to continue to instill your values of integrity and respect.

KEY INSIGHTS

- Show up like a boss—prepared, well dressed, and ready to conquer the day.

- Continue your personal development to expand your leadership capabilities and joy in life.

- Cultivate a mindset of excellence in anything you do, focusing on the effort not the outcome.

- Practice the art of mentorship to encourage respect and integrity in the next generation.

8

VISIT YOUR CLUB MED RETREAT EVERY DAY

The leadership lifestyle habits are the foundations of health, well-being, and emotional resilience. These are what I consider the nonnegotiable habits for truly successful people. Try to build your life above and beyond these foundations. If you find yourself in a situation where you cannot maintain these basic rules of exceptional health and well-being, take time to slow down and reorganize your life.

Try to prioritize these seven foundations that consist of social connection, sleep, nutrition, exercise, gratitude, meditation, and nature whenever possible. Once you understand how these foundations impact your health and capability as a human, you begin to understand that respecting your body and mind is an essential part of joy, prosperity, and success in life and as a leader.

Social Connection

There is no substitute for the benefit of healthy social connections in your life. The ability to feel supported and to support others is a significant part of what makes us human. Evidence exists for the health and longevity benefits of social connection through the research that has been done on the blue zones.

The blue zone research has identified five places around the world where the highest number of disability-free centenarians live, areas such as Okinawa, Sardinia, and Loma Linda. Researchers have identified many commonalities that may contribute to the health and longevity of these populations. Social connection has been identified as a significant factor for all five areas.

Although social media may have been formulated with the idea of connecting people, it seems that the opposite is true. You may have hundreds of friends on social media and yet feel lonely and isolated. In addition, to the loneliness, the increase of constant comparison to idealized lives is increasing levels of depression in the community.

Take the time to cultivate real in-life connections that are critical for your health. You will be able to socialize and to have interactions where you have joy and contentment. These interactions can be powerful to give you an overall sense of well-being. Have a conversation with a close friend during times of difficulty; such connectedness can help you feel, well, connected and supported. Conversely, being the support system for a friend in need can also give you a sense of purpose and closeness with others.

There is a distinct difference between being surrounded by people or having friends on social media than actually connecting to another human. The change in hormones that happens from looking in each other's eyes, the subtle cues that are communicated through facial expressions and body language, and even something as simple as a hug from a close friend or family member can have a significant calming or joyful effect.

When you are setting out to build your business, your time can be constrained and your focus can be driven by the needs of your business. While work is important, close human connections are also important for your overall health and longevity. Focus on the quality over quantity to make sure that you are getting these important opportunities.

Here are some simple suggestions that can help you achieve connection. Schedule lunch with a close friend, even a thirty-minute lunch break on a park picnic table. This simple act of communication and focus on conversation can change your mood. Take a walk or go to the park with your children and actually chase them around and play. Laugh, have fun, look them in the eyes. Let the sense of joy and fun fill you with that wonderful warmth of happiness and gratitude.

In order to focus on the human connection, try to have the quality interactions in ways and places where no distractions keep you from connecting. Turn off the screens, leave your phone in the car, or just turn off the sound. Try to meet in less busy places. Have lunch in a quiet restaurant versus the trendy new lunch place that's hopping. Have friends over for game night once a week. Grab a fun board or card game and talk, laugh, and connect.

It truly can be done to maintain close connections with a tight inner circle of family and friends by focusing on quality even as you build your business. Mini connections can also be had every day as you go through life. Stop looking at your phone or device everywhere you go.

Actually, take the moment to look people in the eye as you are out and about in the day. Say hello and smile to fellow humans that you interact with at the dry cleaners, library, school, and post office. Strike up a conversation about the weather or a trip you want to take and enjoy the interaction. These little boosts of communication and connection can have a grounding effect in this fast-paced, overwhelming world that we face each day.

Sleep

The lifestyle habit of sleep consists of the time and quality of your sleep. Although I have now come to understand how important sleep is to my capabilities, in the world of EMS, sleep was not prioritized. The ability to go for long shifts without sleep was seen as a necessity and being fatigued during a twenty-four-hour shift was seen as a failure.

This type of push from management is seen across many industries these days. People are emailing and texting about work 24/7 and think nothing of it. Unfortunately, for myself and many others, we only find out how wrong this lack of sleep mentality is when we are diagnosed with a significant illness.

As the leader in your life and organization, you have the opportunity to completely change the way you do business. Take on a reverence for the necessity of the human body to get optimal sleep. Now if you are anything like me, you will need some convincing that a required seven to nine hours of sleep a night is truly necessary and not just some weakness or laziness.

Findings from groundbreaking sleep research are indisputable: Sleep is a transformational and required time for the maintenance, learning, and health of the brain and body as a whole.

The research done by Matthew Walker, a neuroscientist and psychologist at the University of California, Berkeley, is life changing. He has spent many years researching the impact that sleep has on our health and well-being as humans. His detailed work and research have led him to publish an excellent book called *Why We Sleep*. Professor Walker is definitely a leader worth following in the area of sleep science, and I encourage you to look more deeply into his information if you are still questioning the need for high-quality sleep every night.

Through his research he has been able to show that the lack of high-quality sleep consistently throughout your life can have significant health consequences. Not only does this increase your chances of obesity by affecting your glucose tolerance and insulin, significant impacts on your hunger patterns and food preferences can also set you up for a daily increase in calorie consumption, which tinkers with how your body is able to deal with those extra calories and sugar. Obesity is one of the top metabolic issues that increases your risk for multiple other disease patterns including diabetes and heart disease, just to name a few.

Other research led the World Health Organization to classify working nights as a probable carcinogen due to sleep deprivation linked to multiple forms of cancer. The impacts of sleep deprivation on the capacity of the immune system are irrefutable. Researchers showed that even one night of reduced sleep has such an impact on the immune system that it can drop up to 70 percent of natural killer cells. This is a marked immune deficiency brought on quickly due to lack of sleep.

If the thought of putting yourself and others at risk for many negative health consequences caused by lack of quality sleep were not enough, other findings point to the negative impacts on mental health. Lack of sleep decreases your ability to have sound judgment and reason as well as increases your risk for anxiety. The idea of burning the midnight oil to run your business is a nonstarter in my book. This research clearly shows that you are better off getting a full night's sleep and then working hard during the day, as a lack of sleep has significant impact on productivity and creativity.

Your brain is at work even during sleep. We need to begin to treat sleep as a required event if we want to be capable of making connections from the information we learn during the day. Different types of sleep patterns affect our ability to solve abstract problems and to commit the information that we learn to our long-term memories. Sleep also allows us to be creative and emotionally stable.

There seems to be a constant drive that more hours of work equal more productivity, but, in reality, that seems to be a long-term recipe for disaster. Work intensely for blocks of time during the day and then allow for optimal sleep, exercise, nutrition, and connection with loved ones. Such habits will increase innovation, creativity, and performance during the hours we are working.

The need for optimizing your sleep is clearly evident through this current research. You can improve your sleep quality in many ways. One area that is clear is that having a consistent sleep routine is critical to the sleep quality. Yep, you guessed it, this means having a bedtime and keeping to it as often as possible even on weekends.

This reminds me of my grandmother's advice that nothing worthwhile happens after dark so you should go to bed at a reasonable time. Maybe there was some wisdom to my grandmother's advice. Maintaining a clearly defined pattern for your circadian rhythm helps you to fall and stay asleep.

Keep the bedroom cool in preparation for your sleep time as a thermal queue for your body to prepare for sleep.

This is used in conjunction with the darkness to allow your body to fall asleep quickly.

There is also a clear recommendation of controlling for the light cycle that is important to maintain the melatonin cycle of the body, which means seeing the sun in the morning and waking hours while downregulating light in the evenings. The last hour before sleep should remain screen-free and in a low-light to no-light state. Use the last hour of the day for reflection or to listen to an audiobook so you can use the time wisely. No screens include no reading on tablets or phones. If you want to read during this hour, make sure to get a real hard copy book and use directed light at the book.

Professor Walker also cautioned against the use of alcohol and marijuana, which he said have negative effects on sleep and therefore health. He also explained that alcohol can lead to fragmented sleep patterns that can be a key factor in unrefreshing sleep. If you are a coffee drinker, you are not off the hook either. He recommended that you do not have any caffeine after noon as this can have a significant impact on your sleep quality.

One point that struck me is that his research showed that if you have significant sleep deprivation in the long term, you actually have a perception change that you begin to feel as if you are okay without the sleep. Although if you actually focused on sleep for a couple of months and maintained optimal sleep, you can reset and begin to feel much better again. The fact that we begin to try and adapt to our sleep-deprived state can actually derail people from prioritizing sleep.

The light cycle is important to your body's regulation of hormones. Your body is diurnal, meaning that we are meant to sleep at night. Many hormones in the body are released and regulated during the sleep time. Make the daily choice to allow for the appropriate light cycle, which will impact the quality of your sleep and your health long term.

I unfortunately learned about this through personal experience. My education began with the diagnosis of a rare neuroendocrine disorder that sent me on a fact-finding mission. As I was educated about the diurnal nature of the human body, I thought back to all the nights I spent working the midnight shift. All of those times I worked the twenty-four-hour shifts only to stay over for an additional twelve hours. This practice of staying awake all night has been normalized in our society with little regard to the natural rhythm of the human body.

Satchin Panda is the leading researcher on the circadian rhythm. His in-depth studies have led to a greater understanding of the intricacies of the human rhythm. Dr. Panda's book, *The Circadian Code: Lose Weight, Supercharge Your Energy, and Transform Your Health from Morning to Midnight*, is a wealth of knowledge on this subject.

As a leader, learn to protect your sleep cycle at all costs. This will have a significant impact on your life and your ability to lead. You may also want to consider how your business or organization can work to protect sleep for your employees as well. Having healthy employees that are innovative and highly productive is a must in our competitive business environment.

Nutrition

Nutrition can affect your leadership lifestyle. The food that we eat has a significant impact on our mood and the health of our bodies and minds. So many conflicting studies are available in this arena. The food debate is intense, and you can find many conflicting guidelines as to what is actually healthy. There does seem to be a consensus in a few areas, so I will stick to that information.

Every day you are faced with massive marketing campaigns that focus on influencing your food choices. The United States has liberal advertising laws with regard to food. If that wasn't enough, just a simple scroll through social media will find image after image of food and recipes. This staggering amount of influence can lead to many missteps in nutrition choices and also contribute to decision fatigue throughout the day.

Meal planning and having healthy food on hand can be a winning strategy for keeping our nutrition on track and decreasing the number of food decisions we are required to make on a daily basis. Instead of putting something as important as nutrition on the typical autopilot, plan ahead and take control of this important leadership lifestyle habit.

Stick to a nutrient-dense diet that includes adequate fat and protein. I am more interested in what should be omitted from the diet in order to avoid negative health impacts. The complete removal of processed foods from the diet can have significant positive results on health and emotional resilience. Highly processed sugar-laden foods can disrupt the body's ability to maintain a stable blood sugar level and can lead to metabolic disorders such as insulin resistance.

Processed foods can have additives, industrialized seed oils, and scent enhancers that lead to food being hyperpalatable and addictive. The increased sugar intake in the diet can lead people to a need to eat frequently to stave off symptoms of sugar withdrawal. Food is an especially important fuel for the body, and this type of vicious cycle can be overwhelming and hurtful to a leader's emotional resilience.

Take control of your nutrition and consider the evolutionary model of the human diet. Our bodies need to be fueled with healthy fats and protein. Fats are slow, long-burning fuels that allow you to not need to constantly snack and be exposed to high-sugar processed food throughout the day. Retrain your brain and body by removing processed foods that can have profound effects on your mood and sense of well-being.

Eat mindfully throughout your day. The availability of food and the fast pace of life can lead you to mindless eating patterns that can impact your health and your waistline. The fact that processed sugar-laden foods are available almost anywhere you go at any time of the day or night can skew your sense of hunger.

Take the time to stop and eat and do nothing else. Do not watch TV, answer emails, or drive while eating. Do not eat on the run. Respect your body and take the five minutes out of your day to be grateful for your food and to pay attention while you eat. Try eating with a friend or family member and just enjoy some exhilarating conversation and happiness.

Just making these small changes will have an impact on your perception of food as a fuel that is important for your mind and body. Now work on learning the importance of physiological hunger versus psychological hunger. With the constant availability of food, our hunger signals can be impacted, so at times eating is done out of habit or craving for sugar and not for true hunger.

If you are not hungry for, say, a steak but you are hungry for ice cream, then you are not actually physiologically hungry. Learn to respect true hunger and then practice gratitude for the healthful meal you eat. You can reshape your relationship with food doing this practice.

Digestion is work for the body. The more processed food and additives that you eat requires your body to detox and digest the large volume of food. The habits of eating at all hours of the day and night can leave your body working on overtime. Respect your body's rest and repair time by leaving a few hours food-free before you jump into bed, which allows your body time to rest and repair during your sleep.

Stay hydrated with water. There is a possibility for your body to confuse the signals of hunger and thirst. Make sure that you give your body the water it needs throughout the day. Keep a water bottle with you at all times to jog your memory. You can always test to see if you are actually thirsty versus hungry by drinking a glass of water before a meal and waiting fifteen minutes to see if you still feel hungry for something nutrient dense and healthy.

For many of us, food is emotional and cultural. Take your time to look at your nutrition and how food is impacting your health and sense of well-being. Work with a nutritional expert if you have questions or complex health needs.

I personally have found that finding a nutrition expert that respects the anthropological view of evolution on human nutrition has had life-changing results for my health and wellness. It has impacted my waistline as well and allowed me to effortlessly maintain my weight loss for years now. Nutrition is a true foundation for life and can affect you on so many levels. Focus on the healthiest unprocessed foods that you can afford. Really make nutrition a priority in your life to develop yourself into the most effective leader you can be.

Exercise

Now that we can see that sleep and nutrition are nonnegotiable, let's consider the next leadership lifestyle habit of exercise. I want to talk about exercise that is required for a sense of well-being, mental clarity, and stress reduction.

No specific exercise plan is able to meet every goal like muscle building or weight loss. Specialized exercise plans are developed to meet different goals by professionals. If you are striving to meet specific body goals with exercise, you should take the time to engage a coach that specializes in those results.

This information is meant to inspire those who have not found a way to include exercise in their regimen. I am not a trainer and will not give you a specific routine. My goal is only to point out some of the ideas about the benefits of adding movement to your daily routine. Please do check with your doctor for any specific advice or medical clearance before implementing a new exercise plan in your life.

Exercise to get your brain working on all cylinders. There can be an immediate change in your mindset and focus just by the simple act of getting up and moving. The midday walk to clear my mind and allow my ideas to percolate has become a staple in my life. This habit happened by chance when my baby would only take a nap in the afternoon if I took him for walks in the stroller. The quiet and exercise quickly began to impact my progress throughout the rest of the day. We both loved our walks.

Exercise does not need to be a zero-sum game. The experts will tell you that so many minutes a day will give you the best impact for your health. This information is amazing, but for some who do not already practice a daily exercise regimen, just the thought of exercise can be overwhelming.

If you want to start an exercise regimen that will stick, just start somewhere. Take a fifteen-minute walk in the afternoon or build up to two a day. Do some simple squats or jumping jacks in the morning to get your blood pumping. I routinely do an entire squat and lunge routine while doing dishes these days. I love the sense of accomplishment it brings me.

The truth about exercise is that if you start slowly and build over time, the benefits of well-being, accomplishment, and cognitive improvements will motivate you to continue. As you continue, you will get better at whatever you are doing.

Choose something you like to do that has minimal barriers to entry. If you like to dance, throw on some music and just dance for a quick fifteen minutes. You are not required to have the perfect workout gear or even leave the house. After you do these mini workouts for a few months and you realize how amazing they can be for your life, you may decide to sign up for a dance class or take up a new hobby that includes exercise.

When you start making the movement an easy-to-do-anywhere nonstressful event, you have the opportunity to build exercise into your life in a way that is fun and enjoyable. The more exercise and movement take hold in your life, the more sophisticated your workouts and results will be, but it all starts with just getting moving.

In your workplace you can build in ways to limit your sedentary atmosphere. They now have all sorts of standing desks and even walking treadmill desks. You could easily arrange for lunch Zumba or a personal trainer to do a quick boot camp for all of your employees. I encourage any leader to think of innovative ways to keep their business up and moving and reap the rewards of a healthy, happy work environment.

Gratitude

This lifestyle habit is what I consider a strategic mental training for contentment. The ability to train your mind to look for the positive in any situation is powerful training for life.

Grateful people are capable of finding the smallest event to be grateful for even in difficult situations in life. This skill trains your brain to find the positive in life and to be content with what you have. After you put this technique into practice, you will find that your brain actually begins to see opportunities to be grateful and productive everywhere, which completely removes a sense of entitlement in your life.

There is no room for entitlement in a leader who practices gratitude daily. Gratitude should be practiced throughout your day as the opportunities present themselves. These can be tiny events for which you take the time to notice and allow yourself to feel happy and thankful—even a beautiful sunrise or a sweet smile from one of your children. Take a second to feel the warmth of gratitude for these amazing moments.

The more you allow this emotion to fill your day, the more your brain will look for other events that allow you to feel that warmth and satisfaction. Your brain will also begin to downregulate the attention to items and situations that you may perceive as negative. This is the ability of neuroplasticity to (re)train your brain.

Practice gratitude before sleep. This is a technique that I have been using for many years, and it has been transformational in my life. I began this practice during a difficult time in my life when I was suffering from chronic illness and was bed bound for a time.

Every evening at bedtime, right before you fall asleep, allow some of the moments of gratitude that you experienced throughout your day to fill your thoughts. Allow the visions to be like pictures in your mind. Allow the flood of emotions and warmth of the feelings to take over. Even allow yourself to smile when you can.

This simple practice will change the way you see the world. Practice this technique just before sleep, which puts you in an amazing relaxed space in preparation for your high-quality night of deep sleep.

Many people also find it a worthwhile practice to journal their items of gratitude during their reflection time. Make a written record that can be looked at in difficult times of life. Whatever method you choose will help you to form these important connections and to strategically train your mind to see the positive in any situation.

Make sure to practice gratitude daily, any chance you can. Smile and accept the gift of beauty in nature or be grateful for the meal that you have to eat. There will begin to be so many experiences and items to be grateful for as you learn to recognize it and appreciate what you have with no comparison to others.

Meditation

The benefits of meditation have been proven over and over again in thousands of scientific studies. Have a daily practice for the process of stress and allow your mind and body to connect. Choose from many different techniques—some are more of a mindful practice and some are more tied to the breath. Whatever you choose to implement in your life, just stick with it.

If you can't find a meditation practitioner to show you a technique (try a yoga class), or if you choose not to seek someone out, then YouTube videos and countless apps can prompt you.

Make a commitment to yourself to show up and meditate, start with seven minutes a day. The more that you stick with it, the more the results in your life will become apparent. For me, meditation has been a grounding experience and allowed me to set intentions for my life and see them become a reality.

As amazing as this practice has been in my life, meditation is the hardest habit for me to follow. The idea of just sitting still for a few minutes trying to "clear my mind" is like a torture session. My mind does not work that way, and the more that I try to stop thinking, the more the thoughts flood my mind.

I have tried many different methods in my search for the benefits of meditation. For me, I need an active form of meditation that keeps my busy mind focused on a task while the body and breath connect. To that end I joined a support group of sorts.

Last year I committed to a year of the Fierce Grace Collective with Annapurna Living (an online private membership group), a collective of women online where we all hold space for each other. I committed to doing the meditation daily even if it was the shorter version. There were days that I did not want to do it. There were days that the thought of the practice seemed overwhelming, but nonetheless I showed up for myself.

This commitment to the group setting was an accountability form for me. The results after the last year were more than I expected, and the support of knowing that others were facing the same challenges in life gave me more strength and resolve to overcome them. My attention to detail and my concentration were enhanced, and my gratitude was increased. I learned to find joy and appreciation for the monotony and the repetitive tasks of daily life.

The Collective is a powerful and positive group of women led by Carrie-Anne Moss. Carrie-Anne is authentic and pure in her delivery of the information. Her genuine approach and knowledge are encouraging yet disciplined. The year was a transformational time following the prompts and direction and listening to the wisdom and committing to the meditation.

Whatever method you choose for meditation, be committed. You don't have to do hours a day to have benefits. Choose a method that you are drawn to. If you have a hard time clearing your mind and just sitting in silence, try a meditation that includes an active component like breath work or a mantra. Just aim to start showing up for the practice every day even when you only have seven minutes. Even this small period of time applied well will allow you to gain the benefits through practice.

When you know that a commitment may be difficult for you, reach out and find a friend for accountability. When life becomes a challenge for you, canceling on yourself is easy. Have a group or accountability partner that can be the extra push to make sure that you show up. This outside pressure can be an effective tool to get you through the adaptation period before a lifestyle practice becomes a well-ingrained habit.

Nature

All around us we have constructed large buildings. These buildings that were once modest structures meant to provide us with shelter and warmth have become prisons. We spend our days locked in cubicles attached to technology. We hurry from place to place in cars only to find comfort locked in our homes at night. The days of being connected to the earth seem to be lost.

As a society we seem to have disconnected with the important role that nature has played in our physical and mental well-being throughout our human evolution. We have even developed a nutritional disorder because of our lack of exposure to the sun. The vitamin D deficit is at epidemic proportions.

Health gurus instruct us to take a vitamin D supplement because of its important role in human health. Almost in the same breath they caution to never let a ray of sun hit your skin and to slather yourself in chemicals to block the sun. You do have to wonder these days if anyone even remembers human history. Vitamin D that is synthesized in the body using cholesterol in conjunction with sunlight on the skin should be a reminder to us as humans that being outside in nature is imperative to our health.

We as humans need to be connected to the earth and disconnected from technology for periods of time. We crave to have direct connection to the people in our lives and to the animals and beauty that grow around us. Allow yourself the time and attention to the earth—an important step to foster healthy leadership and instincts in yourself. Although many health benefits are associated with the practice of reconnecting to nature, I believe the bond is even deeper. A true instinct and intuition comes from returning to this practice.

One thing that is amazing about being a paramedic other than just the autonomy in my work was the freedom of being outdoors every day. Thanks to the system status-posting plan, most paramedics that you see spend their twelve-hour shifts roaming around from place to place. I have posted at hospitals, hotels, beaches, lakes, convenience stores, and many more, frequently out and about walking and interacting with the public to make the shift go by faster. This constant being outside was such a blessing for offsetting the ultimate responsibility that we felt when helping others.

I fear for the younger generation and those that are climbing the corporate ladder. The lack of connection to the earth and each other has led to an increasing loneliness epidemic. There seems to be such a divide as we have turned ourselves into concrete-jungle zoo animals. We have lost that innate sense of what it means to be free. What it means to truly connect and see how we are a part of a system that is greater than ourselves. Gratitude for the earth and the beauty that surrounds us.

Thankfully, we can reincorporate nature into our lives and regain a sense of connectedness to the planet around us every day.

Start simply by adding in a quick fifteen minutes outside in your yard or a local park. You could sit on your patio in the morning and soak up some morning sun while you sip coffee and feel the breeze on your face. Take breaks at work outside and look for a small patch of grass where you can rest your bare feet for a few minutes. All of these simple connections can start to make an impact throughout your life.

I caution people to start slowly initially. Due to the frequent stimulation that has become the norm in our daily lives, some of us can feel a bit of overwhelm when left without technology to distract us. Any time you make a change there is going to be an adjustment period. There may be a discomfort from not looking at your phone. You may have some uncomfortable feelings come up once you quiet the noise in your life.

This is just simply the process of reconnection, and it will take time to become comfortable with your emotions. Of course, as with anything, if you notice that the emotions are too strong or you are having a much more difficult time than you expected, seek out a licensed professional. Any time you as a leader have the opportunity to step out of your comfort zone and allow growth in your life, it will aid in your transformation. Be responsible in getting the professional instruction you need to overcome the challenge.

Amazing areas of nature have been preserved through the state and national parks program. These magnificent representations of this beautiful planet can have a breathtaking ability to recharge your batteries and your soul. I loved watching my young son as he put his small hands on a massive sequoia. I experienced the fascination and wonder about what those trees had seen in the hundreds of years that they had taken to grow and felt the confidence that he too began to feel in seeing that nature had made its way to continue to grow through many challenges.

The beauty that can be found all around us when we look can be inspiring. I am a sucker for the trips to the parks especially since I am a tried and true boy mom.

Whether you are able to get out for a big adventure or you need to stay closer to home, you can incorporate nature into your life. Start simple with lovely plants that you can grow indoors or right outside to see every day. I have a few lavender plants they are so fragrant and calming. I love having a small rosemary bush. They are hearty and smell amazing all year long. They do well inside, and as a bonus you can use them for cooking.

We have a bird feeder in our front yard that brings in so many animals. I love to stay busy washing dishes watching our resident squirrel defend the bird feeder from the many species of birds that come to grab a bite. These are always fun interactions that can completely take your stress away and change the monotony of dishwashing into an entertaining and somewhat meditative activity.

Wherever you live, look for an opportunity to include a small bit of nature into your daily routine.

 **KEY INSIGHTS**

- Social connection is an important part of developing as a leader and maintaining emotional resilience.
- Sleep is a necessity for the human body and should be prioritized daily. Establish your nightly bedtime routine and stick to it.
- Nutrition is the fuel that allows your body and emotions to function at their peak.
- Gratitude is a strategic practice for increasing joy and fulfillment in your life. Be grateful for the small opportunities every day.
- Meditation is an opportunity to connect the mind and body daily. This practice of connection will help to increase awareness and attention to detail.
- Nature and the connection to our planet is a critical component for overall health and well-being. Spend time in nature every day and allow the breathtaking beauty to inspire you.

9

KEYS TO COMMAND

Daily Strategic Contemplation

The amount of information that is consistently greeting us throughout our days seems to have edged out the simple act of daily strategic contemplation. This is a true tragedy for leadership.

The art of contemplating interactions that we have throughout our days trains our brain to think strategically and allows us to respond and execute even in stressful situations requiring a quick response. This is like an athlete training daily for their sport as they practice. They continue to improve. For you as a leader the daily art of strategic contemplation will allow you to train for difficult times. Practice definitely makes perfect, so you want to commit yourself to this practice daily.

To do the daily strategic contemplation, start with fifteen to thirty minutes a day. I try to shoot for an hour if serious situations or decisions have been going on in life. Just do the best that you can to make contemplation a habit that you do every day.

Practice in a calm, quiet environment without distraction. Now begin by reviewing an interaction or decision that you made during your day. Initially take the time to acknowledge any of the activities that you did well. Think about how your actions helped to shape the interaction or the decision. Take note of the skills that you used in the interaction.

Now review the areas of the interaction or decision that did not go the way you would have liked. Consider what happened. What would you have done differently? Do you have the skills or knowledge that you need to make the changes? Do you need to consult an expert or look something up to give you the skills to make the changes that you would have liked to have made? This is a really significant opportunity to prepare for the next time you have this type of interaction.

This is also the ideal time to have your journal out and ready. Use this opportunity to journal the actions that you need to learn or strategies that you are working on. Make notes for yourself so that you can follow up on the information that you elucidated from this practice. Ensure that you look up any information that you need to learn or work to develop skills that you are lacking.

Finally, visualize the whole interaction with an eye to implementing the changes that you would have made. Visualization and practical application of strategy is like cementing this information in your brain to use the next time you have a similar interaction or decision. The simple act of daily strategic contemplation will have a significant impact on your ability to execute in the future. This process also allows you to gain skills, counsel, and information to increase your skill and knowledge as a leader.

Avoid the pitfall of rumination when using strategic contemplation. This method is not about beating yourself up over mistakes that were made. This is not about a consistent rumination over an event. The point of this review and contemplation is to train your mind and gain skills for future interactions.

If you come across a situation that keeps playing over in your head and you are unable to move on, seek out an expert, which is always a smart idea. Strong leaders know that asking for help and using the abilities of experts is important to maintaining your ability to lead. Leadership, as I have said, is a huge responsibility, and making the hard calls can be emotionally difficult. There is no shame in seeking help from an expert in psychology or human behavior.

After you have been practicing your strategic contemplation for a consistent period of time, you will notice a change. You will become more strategic in your thought process. You will be more confident in your decisions, which will allow you to be decisive with others. You will also look for ways that you can improve your skill sets and information with every challenge you face. These are excellent skills to build in developing yourself as a leader.

Strategic Response

Today, it seems that rapid fire reaction via Twitter or some other version of social media has become the norm. A lack of strategic planning is involved with this type of reaction. The last thing you want to do as a leader is react in a knee-jerk fashion without considering the outcome of your decisions or comments.

This atmosphere alone has changed the way many communicate and interact with others. But do not allow this to dictate the way you communicate. I often ask people if they would have been able to make the same comment or reaction in public as they posted on Facebook, for example. What if they were in public with the person standing face-to-face with them? Usually, the answer is a resounding no.

The perceived anonymity that people feel as they rapid fire from their couch has degraded our public discourse. People feel entitled to their comments no matter how ill-informed they are.

The need for well-planned strategic responses has never been more essential in our society. The need for respect and an ability to maintain civility in our public discourse is apparent daily. The ability to respond confidently with respect is part of winning the long game for leaders. Getting in a comment or dig is easy because it really takes little skill to put almost anyone in their place these days. Leadership should set the example and require more of ourselves and those on our business team.

When you are responsible for others in a leadership position, you must remain emotionally tempered and strategic in any responses that you give. This also includes any interaction that you may have with the public as your customers and your employees. Leaders who react instead of respond strategically degrade the loyalty and respect of their employee base. For this reason, it is important to consider when a response is even required.

Is the situation one that requires a response such as a business partner request or customer complaint? Does the situation have a legal requirement for your business? Do you believe the situation will have a negative impact on your business reputation? These are just a few questions that you can use to decide the type of response that will be required.

Many situations do not even rise to the level of giving a response. Often taking the high road of silence can be the most respectable position. When a response is required, continue to remain professional. Unless there is a life-or-death situation that requires an immediate response, or if you are unsure what your response should be, I always recommend sleeping on it. Allow time and strategic reflection to guide you.

For you as a leader, a calm and capable sense of emotional resilience is the ideal skill to have. Think about the people who get highly emotional and react to everything that happens. These people become like the leader that cries wolf. The ability to stay calm and strategic during difficult times allows you to inspire confidence and trust in your employees and customers.

When you do on occasion raise your emotional state, then it may be obvious to people that the temperature has changed, and your heightened reaction will be highly effective in a crisis situation to motivate people to act.

Developing emotional resilience and temperance takes time and dedication. It requires a consistent review of your personal interactions and a deliberate plan to change areas that need improvement.

Remove any alcohol and drugs, which can definitely have huge impacts on your body and mind and will contribute significantly to your ability to maintain sound judgment and emotional resilience at all times. Although we live in a society that is highly addictive, and we have normalized the frequent use of drugs and alcohol, you need to decide how important being a leader worth following is to you. This is about the performance of your body and mind. This is about your capacity to respond as a leader at any time, day or night.

Command Presence

Late night, and the moon is high in the sky. You are driving home on the freeway when out of nowhere your car is struck and you are spinning out of control. When you come to a stop, the windshield glass is fragmented around you and the smoke from the airbag is disorienting. This chaotic scene with people shouting and cars flying by is a nightmare for all involved.

I know. I was at many of these scenes as a paramedic.

In the moment of considerable despair, you hear a calming voice outside your window. The calming, secure voice asks, "Are you okay? We are going to get you out of there."

The distinct confidence of the first responder brings with it a sense of calm direction and safety.

The ability of the paramedic to give clear, decisive direction and maintain the calm tone of voice allows you to relax and gives a sense of order to a situation that just moments before was overwhelming and out of control. Command presence is an elusive skill that can be indescribably effective during any chaotic or stressful environment.

Command presence is a calm, strong, and decisive demeanor. Command presence is not bossy, rude, or dismissive. In the midst of a crisis, command presence in the leader is a skill that allows for precision and well-executed directions. The command presence will change the tone of the crisis and allow for progress where disorganized inefficiency was before.

The command presence must include a decisive and direct component. Learning to take in all information, as I discussed before, and then making a decision and feeling confident in that decision is exceedingly important in getting others to follow your direction.

When leaders are not confident in their direction during a crisis, employees or bystanders may choose not to follow the direction. "Do this, um, no, I mean do that" in an unsure tone can lead to your team questioning everything that you tell them to do. They may lack confidence in your ability to lead. They may choose to do something completely different, leaving you, the leader, unaware that the success of your crisis plan is in jeopardy. Give calm and decisive direction with your low-tone commander voice to communicate strength, and you'll eliminate this threat.

A skilled leader with a composed and strong command presence can take a completely chaotic, traumatic environment (in my case, an accident scene or a tragic fall or gunshot scene) and almost immediately change the situation to an ordered environment. Not everyone is comfortable in this role, but the exciting news is that this is a trainable skill. Learn to make decisions and stick with them as a first step in developing your command presence.

Remember that the command presence should be a calming force in any chaotic situation. Speaking in a low-tone voice is important especially if everyone else is in total flip-out mode. Your low and direct commander voice will set the tone for your employees and customers.

Learn to shift your body into an expansive position as you develop your leadership command presence. Important work on the power of posture has been done by Amy Cuddy, a social psychologist who earned her doctorate from Princeton. Her studies have shown that in this area you can actually fake it until you make it. She has developed information that shows that the pose that you take actually changes your confidence and response in any situation. This is exciting especially for leaders who find command presence in challenging situations difficult.

Dr. Cuddy's studies have shown that expanding your body changes your sense of confidence. The act of changing your posture can actually change how powerful you feel. When people contract their posture, they begin to feel less powerful and fearful. You can apply the work that she has done when preparing to handle crisis situations by spending as little as two minutes alone practicing a power pose to increase your confidence and gain a sense of authentic power. A power pose as she demonstrates can be as simple as standing in a Wonder Woman–type stance with broad shoulders and hands on hips. The power is in the expansion of the body to become bigger and therefore stronger. Her book, *Presence: Bringing your Boldest Self to Your Biggest Challenges*, has many exciting insights into how her work can be applied to life.

When you are faced with an overwhelming challenge or business crisis, you will fall to the level of your training. For this reason, practicing regularly with high-value training is important. Daily practice of the mindset of excellence, giving your full effort to even the small aspects and the daily strategic contemplation visualization, will help you to be prepared for just these events. The ability to slow down previous interactions and challenges and walk through how you want them to go will help you to be ready to do that in real time.

The daily practice of bringing your best effort to every situation will help to prepare you for when that effort really counts. Make sure that you are the leader that is prepared for challenges.

While training paramedics, I always felt that it was important for them to know what to do when they were unsure of what to do. For this purpose, I always trained them how to consult their protocol book or contact their base physician if they were hesitant to act in a crisis situation. The practice of their finding the answer themselves instead of my just giving it to them ensured that if this event arose after they were out on their own, they would know what to do.

It would have been easy to give them the answer. Instead, while they had the support and someone to manage the critical patient for them, I taught them the importance of actually doing the skill, of looking it up or making contact themselves. I had complete confidence that when the need arose, after they had graduated, they would be completely capable of performing these tasks in stressful situations.

The training for what to do in the moment of crisis or challenge is extremely important for the leader. Every business will face challenges at some point, and knowing that gives you the opportunity to practice your daily strategic contemplation and gain knowledge and skills. The practice of visualizing the application of those skills while changing the outcome of the situation is excellent practice for the real crisis.

Learn to stay calm and focused in chaos. Take deep breaths and count to ten before responding can be a simple yet effective tool for regrouping and slowing your speech and lowering your tone of voice. You can and should build your command presence as a skill that will allow you to effectively direct and overcome the challenges that you will face.

Hindsight Is 20/20

When you firmly take your leadership position, you will find that the criticism and analysis of others can be quite harsh. It never ceases to amaze me that others who have the benefit of time and the resource of knowing the outcome think they would have performed better in the moment.

Of course, any time you are able to sit and think through a decision with the outcome already decided, you have the ability to point out the areas that could have changed the outcome. This is why we practice the strategic contemplation. The better you get with your visualization, strategic planning, and walk-through, the more confident you will become in your decision-making in real time.

As a leader you must develop a thick skin. There will always be those individuals who should have, would have, or could have done something different. Great. Hopefully everything is working out successfully in their business. Do not let this type of talk get to you. Wish them well and do the best you can in the future situations that you face.

Accept constructive criticism that helps you to perform better in the future. Remain coachable and allow yourself to learn from others. Just make sure that the person who is giving you advice is in a position to teach you versus just being a naysayer.

Ah, the naysayers. They seem to come out in droves to kick you whenever you are down. Some are so discontented in life that they will go out of their way to bring you down. Stay focused. Do not allow the haters to bring you down. Try to align yourself with other leaders who are working toward excellence themselves.

Always be willing to evaluate situations that did not have the outcome that you were expecting. Use the opportunity to learn and prepare for the future challenges you will face. Never miss an opportunity to learn and grow in your leadership position.

The leaders who develop strategic intuition are people who learn more from failure or mistakes then they do from success. The development of strategic intuition is a blending of knowledge, wisdom, and life experience. Without mistakes and learning, you will be unable to build this important skill while moving through your leadership journey.

KEY INSIGHTS

- Cultivate the practice of daily strategic contemplation; train your brain for strategic evaluation and tactical execution in your daily leadership role.

- Strategic response is necessary when in the leadership role and should be maintained by developing emotional resilience, while using sound judgment. Think before you respond.

- The elusive skill of command presence should be a key ability to develop in the leadership position. This skill that inspires confidence and calm in difficult situations can be a leader's secret weapon.

- Hindsight is always 20/20. Use your ability to remain coachable and seek mentors when necessary. Happily, move the naysayers along when necessary.

10

FOCUS YOUR LENS LIKE PAPARAZZI

Feeling Triggered?

Everywhere I turn I hear the term *feeling triggered*. This is an interesting perspective that people seem to be wearing like a badge of honor. That somehow their emotional state is to be praised. Leadership should not be triggered.

If you allow your buttons to be pushed or you have a change of your emotional state due to a situation, you give away your power. You have now allowed someone else or a situation to take charge of your emotions. This is a negative as a leader and nothing to be proud of in any way.

We as leaders need to be responsible for our emotional states, as I discussed earlier in building emotional resilience. If you are having issues that are triggering you, then you need to work to resolve those in some way that is strategic and productive. Of course, for any situation that you feel is deeply rooted in personal trauma or tragedy, you should seek professional expertise to help you make the optimal progress.

We can never control situations that happen around us, but as leaders we can work on the way that we respond and use these events within our own lives. Mental health professionals can give leaders the tools to move forward from these events.

Other situations that trigger you may not require professional support but still need to be worked through so that you can maintain your emotional resilience and calm and your sense of personal power. These situations are an important place to use your skill of strategic contemplation. Consider what about the situation triggered you. What aspects of the situation went well? What are some ways that you could get involved? In what way could you have reacted differently? Make sure that you do a positive strategic visualization so that you are prepared to downregulate your sense of being triggered in the future.

When opportunities for you to be involved or to volunteer to make changes in your local community become available, show up. Take the opportunity to be a part of change and to see the faces of the people you can help. You as a leader will have the opportunity to feel a sense of accomplishment and gratitude. Your volunteering will make a difference to the people of your community and can really fuel a sense of pride for your business and your team as a whole.

The Leadership Lens

How you view the world informs your perception. As the leader, learn to focus and expand your lens. That's a trainable skill. When you are the leader, you will be interacting with people from all walks of life. They will be from different cultures and represent many age groups. People's perspectives are usually informed by their way of life and upbringing.

This training of your leadership lens is about learning to see the world from multiple vantage points. It's interesting how information and explanations can be changed when they come from different directions or vantage points. Use this exercise to learn to evaluate your interactions and situations from different vantage points. Changing your perspective can be impactful on your perception of the world and individuals.

Train your mind for the neutral lens. So much information is available today. Information can come from many different sources, and it can be easy to quickly develop an opinion. The neutral lens is used to take in information and not attach a positive or negative to the information until you have gathered all the facts needed. Have an open mind and take in information. This strategy will make or break you in many decisions that you make.

Remember that kindhearted people who really want to see other people succeed still thrive. These people go out of their way to help you and to advise you the best they can. On the flip side are definitely people who truly do not have positive intentions and will take you for everything you are worth.

Learn to take in information in this neutral way, which can help you to develop your instincts to recognize the positive information versus negative information.

The neutral lens will also help you learn to gain all the facts and perspectives that can help you make strong tactical decisions. Sometimes the best ideas will come from the most surprising places. Learn to hear people out without forming an opinion.

This will allow you to stop trying to read into someone's intent. No longer will you immediately try to speculate whether someone meant something negative or was upset by you. You will gather all of the information and work based on facts. Train your mind to remain neutral until the facts are in. The neutral lens is a powerful technique in your personal and professional life.

Practice will increase your ability to use the neutral lens in all situations. Don't be discouraged if it takes a while to develop. When you start with a negative view, ask yourself why you feel negative about the situation. Was there information that you felt intuitively or were you just feeling vulnerable in the moment? This analysis and reframing of the situation will allow you to get back on track with the neutral lens protocol.

Tunnel vision—the inability to see because of a myopic perspective—can be detrimental to you as a leader. Looking at a situation in such a closed-minded way decreases the options that you have. When you look at a problem or a situation without considering all the factors that may have contributed to the problem, it can change the way you would respond.

Think of a camera that is focused in tightly for a picture. Maybe you see items and people up close, but if you zoom out, you have the opportunity to see that the context of the situation has completely changed. In a tsunami you may see a low tide on the beach and people running. As you zoom out, you begin to see the huge tidal wave that is threatening the town. This is an extreme example, but tunnel vision can really hamper you as a leader.

This camera focus practice can be effective in training your mind to be more observant and consider many differing views throughout your day. Practice thinking outside the frame. Consider the perspective of others who are in the situation.

The more that you take the time to practice this technique, the more efficient you will become at seeing each situation from many vantage points, which will allow you to process information quickly and change the way you plan your strategy for success.

Another way that you can enhance your leadership strategic planning is through the use of filters in your camera focus review. The application of filters when logically thinking through the frame can help to determine options and steps that could be used in upcoming situations. Consider the idea of using a filter of compassion when reviewing a situation with an employee or customer. Consider using the warrior mentality filter when facing a difficult challenge or problem.

Consider the use of the fixer filter when you need to deal with a significant problem that needs to be resolved.

Use these different mindsets to evaluate and reframe situations as you develop strategic planning capabilities. This trainable skill becomes more effective in real time the more that you practice it in a safe reviewing manner.

Communication

I believe that leadership has a responsibility to always maintain an authentic and honest perspective in every interaction. While honesty is paramount, the presentation of the information is tailored based on the person who will be receiving the information. You can categorize people into one of four groups when determining how you will formulate your communication.

Know who you are talking to and tailor your communication appropriately. There are times when what you said may not be as important as how you said it. In my former life, the medics would often laugh about the ability of some care providers to endear themselves to the patients. This ability would make the patients believe that the provider would never do them harm. Having that feeling toward the care provider almost always ensured a safety of sorts from liability. Not because of the care that was provided necessarily but because of the communication of caring that the patient received.

Learn to always tell the truth but modulate the presentation of the truth to match the situation; then you can deliver difficult news when necessary. Let's face it, telling people exceptional or positive news is always easy and something to look forward to. Only in those moments where a hard truth will need to be delivered is this skill going to be a secret weapon for you as a leader.

I have learned to organize people into four categories to appropriately develop the way that I communicate. Take many factors into consideration when developing a strategy for communicating with others, including their level of expertise and your leadership power over them. Know how you relate to people, which will inform your delivery of a message, because not all individuals will receive information in the same way based on these factors.

These four categories are equals, experts, neutrals, and employees. Although not all rules are hard and fast for the individuals that you will encounter, these categories can guide you in the importance of delivering your message in a manner that will help it to be well received.

> **Equals:** These are people who do not work in your organization. They are people with similar education and age group that feel as if they are on fair footing when interacting. This is a group where there is an opportunity to have true and objective conversations. You can let your guard down because these are the people in your personal inner circle—you may allow yourself to be vulnerable with them. This is a group that will expect your pure,

honest interpretation when they ask for advice. There is no sugar-coating required in any communication here.

Experts: These are people that I am getting advice from that are specialists in their fields. They are lawyers, accountants, and other professionals. In this area of communication, remain coachable and be ready to take advice and counsel.

Neutral: These are people that you meet in your day-to-day life that you have minimal interaction with or knowledge of. You may interact with them in the grocery store or at your child's school. This could also include your customer base. Maintain a professional and upbeat demeanor whenever possible. With your neutral group you can practice your ability at kind small talk. These are the people where the old saying goes: If you have nothing nice to say, then say nothing at all.

Employee: It is important to recognize when a person sees you as the authority. Whenever you are in a position of authority or power, you need to be careful about how you communicate. People can easily react in a negative way especially if they feel that their livelihood is threatened. This can be stressful and people can overreact. Even if the information that you have to share is negative, because that is the truth, present this information in a kind and direct manner. Showing compassion and consistency will help during these types of difficult interactions.

Interpersonal communication in the work environment can be tricky. There will be situations where you have made decisions that make people unhappy. There will be tough times where it becomes necessary to correct negative behavior of an employee. All of these situations will require you as the leader to maintain a strong yet compassionate form of communication. Take the time to hear out employees. People need to feel heard and validated over their concerns, even if you are unable to change the situation.

When delivering criticism or hard news to employees, make sure to frame the message in positive and compassionate ways. Although you may need to be direct, you never want an employee to feel attacked. You want to encourage employees to do better because they are a part of the team. Although they may need to change a behavior in that moment, you want them to succeed and move forward with your team.

Part of the message that you need to deliver clearly with your employee base are your expectations, values, and policies. There should be no surprises for employees about what is expected in your work environment. Not only should they clearly understand the expectations, but they should also know exactly what the consequences are if they choose not to follow them. Consistency in the leadership when dealing with discipline is important for team morale and cohesion. Do not play favorites among your employee base if you want to have a successful business. This advice extends to your personal communications as well.

Learning to communicate is a necessity as a leader. Communication includes much more than just what you say. You also need to do active listening and work on your body language. Sometimes your nonverbal communication can say more than your words. Actions can speak even louder than anything you may say. If you are not a skilled communicator, definitely sign up for some communication classes or grab some books on the subject. This is a skill that every leader should put in their tool kit.

Failure as a Launchpad

In a world where there is a record number of entrepreneurs and new business owners, a significant number of businesses will fail. Although being excited about the opportunity of stepping out on your own is useful, there is also a real risk that your business may fail.

Many factors can contribute to the possibility of success and failure. Some situations may be out of your control, and, in others, they may be a direct result of decisions made by the leader. Either way, being prepared for the risk and reward that comes with leadership is important.

Some individuals are completely paralyzed by the risk of failure. They will make decisions digging themselves in deeper and deeper doing anything to avoid what they view as a failure. In the end they have such a huge failure in their vision that they have a difficult time recovering from the situation.

Failure is inevitable in leadership. I have never spoken to a leader who is successful in the long term who has not had failures along the way. In my own path to leadership, there have been many failures and course corrections. In the moment those failures were difficult and painful, but they were also transformational. These moments are where I learned the most and built an inordinate amount of personal grit. Without the failures in my life, I would never be writing this book nor would I have returned to school to complete my master's degree in leadership. These failures were truly a launching pad for me in my life.

We as leaders need to change how we look at what we perceive as failure. The only true failure that I see is one in which you learn nothing. If a plan falls apart and you do not accomplish your goal but you learn invaluable lessons and build personal resolve, then you have not failed. You have received a real-life lesson to move forward. Take what you learn and keep moving forward.

The naysayers will always be in the background. There will always be those who will criticize and be willing to give you their opinion. Please shut out the noise. The fact that you have a passion to be a leader and you want to move forward in your life is amazing. If every leader who was criticized or told that they couldn't do this or that stopped, our world would be totally different.

Take the fear out of failure by being up front with yourself that you may fail. You may have to change course while developing your business. Knowing this up front and doing it anyway is the true definition of courage. Know that all of the challenges you face will serve to sharpen your skills and build your personal resolve. Know that steel is forged in fire and amazing leaders are as well.

KEY INSIGHTS

- Emotional temperance is a hallmark for strong leadership. Take control of emotions that would make you feel triggered today.

- Communication is a highly valued skill for leaders. Use the method of categorizing people to help you formulate an effective communication strategy.

- Failure can be your strongest teacher in life. Recognize that failure only exists when there is nothing to be learned from the situation.

11

SPEED BUMPS, POT HOLES, AND RABBIT HOLES

Use That Knowledge to Win

Knowledge is of no use to anyone who does not apply it to their lives. Take action. Don't wait for an invitation to make this knowledge a part of your life. Take the initiative to build a life you love.

I have presented a lot of information in this book to help you become the best leader you can be. Take your time to begin to apply these strategies and lifestyle habits. When we want our changes to stick, we need to take the time to allow them to become automatic habits in our life.

Your different personality traits can influence how you tackle making changes in your life. Some of us prefer to make small, slow, deliberate changes, and others prefer the cold turkey all-in method for change. Respect your natural inclination to make changes in the way that suits you and apply the knowledge. Allow the knowledge and daily practice to develop you into your best self.

To continually improve yourself and reach new goals should be a life's work. Once you reach a new level of personal development, you will be able to see new ways in which you can continue to improve or add to your skill set. This lifelong pursuit of your best self in conjunction with living your purpose will give you the opportunity to live a joyful, contented life of discipline and purpose.

No One's Friend—Procrastination

Every leader is faced with situations they are not excited to deal with. Procrastination in and of itself is a learned behavior, and there are ways to combat this head on. Procrastination can have negative and stressful impacts on your life. It can affect your performance of tasks when you shorten the window to complete them. Have a plan for every day as an initial step in mitigating the urge to procrastinate.

Start with an assessment of the activities that you are procrastinating about. Is the feeling of drudgery or overwhelm warranted? Is there a pattern of the tasks that you don't want to do? Do you feel overwhelmed by a large project? Is there a difficult conversation that needs to be managed? Identifying the reason that you are wanting to put off the situation will help define a plan to overcome the procrastination behavior.

Once you have identified why you are feeling overwhelmed by the problem at hand, the time has come to overcome the barriers to success. If you find that you need to make a difficult decision or have an interaction that is troubling you, make contact with a mentor or expert in that area.

Take the time to receive advice from someone who has experience with similar situations. Don't just talk it over with a friend. Actually, seek out some valuable, experienced advice to prepare you for the interaction or to help you make the decision.

Practice your strategic contemplation as a visualization for the interaction. Walk it through by paying attention to the key points that you want to include. Spend the time focusing on how your demeanor stays calm and, on your capability, to get your points across while directing the interaction. This visualization is your practice round for the main event.

Preparing in this way will not only ready you for the conversation or interaction, but will help to downregulate your sense of nervous energy. This is training your subconscious that this interaction is safe and calm by visualizing the interaction in a nonthreatening place and maintaining a calm, patterned breathing. Take the time to visualize the interaction a few times so that you are calm and confident for the real thing.

If you are procrastinating because you are overwhelmed at the size of a project or the amount of work that you have, let's break it down. Rome was not built in a day, and some tasks can feel daunting when you consider the entire big picture. Instead, let's take the time to break the task into achievable steps.

Once you have segmented the task by steps, focus on just completing one task at a time. Just keep showing up and putting one foot in front of the other, and soon you will be completed with what was once an overwhelming prospect.

Consistency is key in training your brain to overcome procrastination. This seems to be a resounding theme throughout life—that the more you are consistent, the more reliable the results that you receive. I recommend a strong commitment to facing the situation that is causing you to procrastinate in a timely manner. Whenever possible, I will tackle any project or situation that I'm not looking forward to first and just clear it off my to-do list.

Having items on your to-do list that you are dreading will inevitably impact all of your other interactions throughout the day. They will cause stress and strain that is completely unnecessary, as usually the anticipation of the interaction is far worse than the outcome. "Worrying is like paying a debt you don't owe," Mark Twain said. He went on, "I have spent most of my life worrying about things that have never happened."

Put procrastination in the past if you practice these steps. The commitment to tackle tasks that you aren't looking forward to first in the day will give you a sense of control over challenging situations. Set the example for your employees that when you have a difficult problem or situation, you show up and face it head on. This mindset will encourage your employees to follow your lead and do the same.

What to Do When You Don't Know What to Do

There will be times in your life and leadership role where you feel stuck. You may even feel as if you don't know what to do. When these situations arise, meet them head on with the warrior mindset. Know that you will figure it out and move on to the next chapter of life. This is an important first step in the process of figuring out your next best step.

When you don't know what to do, first determine your timeline. Is this a situation that requires a quick response, or do you have time to come up with a strategic plan for execution?

Consult an expert in the area where you are feeling stuck. Sometimes you just need some fresh eyes and someone to point you in the right direction to get you over the hump and back on track. Experts often use many different techniques for overcoming all kinds of challenges, and their experience and knowledge can be invaluable. It may take a simple phone call to an expert to find out that they have faced this challenge with clients previously and they can easily walk you through the obstacle.

Talk it through with a mentor that has experience and can give you sound advice. Take the time to go through the pros and cons of the situation. Apply all the facts and the resources you have to develop a strategic plan and then put it into action and move forward. Never just leap or make a hasty decision; instead, use your knowledge and plot steps to determine the best course of action.

When all else fails, start with the basics. Sleep on it and allow your brain to form connections and consider the outcomes. Work out and build up a sweat so that you feel more powerful and calm. Let those endorphins work while you are pushing through. Finally, fuel your body and mind with sound nutrition so that your mind has all the fuel it needs to make the best decision.

Now you will know what to do. Once you have devised your plan, take action.

Food for Thought

Leadership gives you an amazing opportunity to innovate as you move forward in your business. There is a wisdom in respecting the ideas and systems of those that came before you in your industry. Amazing information can be gleaned in the structures and philosophies of our elders.

As a leader you have a responsibility to those you lead to not only know and understand these intricacies but also to contribute to the way situations are handled. The answer that is routinely given for why we do things is, this is the way it has always been done. To me this answer no longer cuts the mustard. We as leaders have the responsibility to improve the environment and other factors that affect our businesses and employees.

Have you considered ways that you can step outside of the box to change the way you do business? Have you considered other pathways? As the leader you will have the opportunity to make change and to define new paths for old problems. When you see what needs to be changed for the health and well-being of your team, break the task down step-by-step. Why is it that we do this procedure this way? What was the old way of thinking and why?

Determine areas where you can make change and be willing to monitor these changes for any unintended consequences that may arise. Know where decisions came from and understand as many historical principles as possible, which can help you to develop an out-of-the-box plan without repeating mistakes of others.

Technology and the Rabbit Hole

As the leader in your life and business, your ability to focus and be efficient is essential. You need to be able to think outside the box and respond when necessary. This ever-increasing technological environment has significant impact on your ability to think deeply and concentrate.

I am grateful for technology and am in no way advocating moving back to the prairie lifestyle. Believe me when I tell you I love my washer and dryer. These advancements make my life so much easier. There is a difference between technologies that we use to accomplish certain types of tasks. These appliances and equipment free us to create and do the important interactions and experiences in life.

The technology that seems to have deleterious effects on our brains and emotions are the ones that are constantly distracting or overstimulating our minds and emotions. The consistent nature of the applications and emails to alert you constantly not only breaks your concentration but can also completely change your mood depending on what information you are directed to.

Let's say you're having a productive day and working hard and all of a sudden you get an alert from CNN about a traumatic news story. That notice can completely change how you are able to accomplish your work. You do not need to know instantly about every terrible thing that happens across the globe. How does the information that is routinely breaking your concentration and changing your emotional state impact you as the leader of your own life?

The underlying pressure that you are missing something or you need to react every time you have a like or comment increases an overall artificially anxious environment. We live in a heavily marketed environment that creates a constant undertone of pressure to buy or do or miss out. This alone can decrease your ability to maintain deep thought or find your creativity. As the leader you need to train your mind to maintain calm and clear focus.

Many different techniques can help you on your mission to increase your effective thought and creativity. Take time to just be quiet and allow your mind to actually think and roam where it will. Allow the stimulation to come from the internal source of your mind. Know that only a few situations in which you need to immediately jump into action will happen. In fact, just that feeling that you need to constantly be ready to spring into action causes your cortisol or the stress hormone to remain elevated, which can negatively impact functions like sleep and digestion and increase your body's workload.

Take a moment to just realize that missing out on a post about a new cat video or amazing meal or vacation spot is okay. Missing out may be the best thing that ever happens to your sense of contentment and your ability to not only be efficient but to excel where others fail.

Freely give your mind and body the time to focus on all of the amazing neural connections and creativity that you have inside of you. Protect your mind by giving it quality stimulus in a measured way so that your brain can actually process and apply the knowledge.

Release the need to be involved in every aspect of life and just focus on the most important areas of your life. The more that you take control of how you allow technology to impact your life, the better the results you will have.

There is nothing more freeing than just unplugging from technology. I do this daily and allow my mind to be filled with ideas and plans. Downregulating the control and stimulation from a constant pressure has allowed me the freedom to continue my education, spend time with my family, and expand my business by writing this book. These opportunities would never have been possible if I allowed my day to be constantly interrupted and my mind hijacked.

Turn off your devices and take a sabbatical from the constant need to check in. Read books that will enhance your knowledge in an area that you want to improve. Take a class to learn to ballroom dance or even just let yourself sneak in an afternoon nap. Taking the time to feed your soul and listening to your own voice will enhance your life in many ways.

Your ability to concentrate and find new, ingenious ways to tackle problems will come to you. When you do sit down to do work, your mind will be focused and that constant sense of pressure and fear of missing out will be downregulated. Try it and take your leadership to a whole new level.

Now, on the other hand, this advice does not necessarily apply to your business life where you may need to have a succinct and detailed social media plan to grow your business. Although social media can be effective in raising awareness for your business, you still need to be the leader and decide how you will use this tool. Stop letting the tail wag the dog. You set the times and ways in which you will engage social media platforms.

In this business strategy the same rules apply. Check and respond to social media only in designated times and preplan your posts once a week. You do not need to spend hours a day getting lost in the social media rabbit hole to grow your business. Think of social media as a tool that you use for your benefit, not as a job that you are required to check in with.

No Excuses the Viking Way

Life is full of challenges, and it can be downright hard. Everyone that you talk to who has found success in their life has had to focus, work hard, and push through. There will be times in your life where you have to decide who you are. Are you going to be the person who lies down and gives up? Leaders stand up and push through like Vikings, no excuses. This is when you find out what you are made of. In these moments of true adversity and challenge, you will strengthen your will.

When situations start to get hard, take the opportunity to recognize that these challenges will pass. Don't give yourself a free pass to fail. Leaders brainstorm for solutions to challenges and implement plans for success.

Reevaluate the situation to see if you need to make course changes in your plans or just keep pushing through. Don't make excuses to yourself for why you don't need to succeed. The defeatist attitude is not the way of the strong leaders. Put on your Viking warrior filter and push through with true perseverance. You are always so much stronger than you know. When you feel as if you have nothing left, you will find that you have a reserve and you are just getting started.

A Final Thought

As you move forward on your journey to becoming a tried and true leader, use this information to inspire yourself to face challenges head on. Take the techniques and mindset shifts that you have learned and apply the knowledge in your life to improve your capability while maintaining your joy and contentment.

Your ability to become strategic in your thought process and to remain emotionally resilient will empower you. Stay true to your vision and align your daily actions. This will allow you to meet not only your professional goals but also your personal ones. Tony Robbins said it best when he said that "success without fulfillment is the ultimate failure."

Take this information and use it to safeguard your ability to find fulfillment and professional success in your life.

KEY INSIGHTS

- Knowledge in and of itself is not powerful. Only when you apply knowledge in your life does it become a powerful tool. Take the opportunity to apply knowledge daily to become a leader who wins.

- Procrastination is a learned behavior that can be overcome by implementing simple techniques. Don't let dread and overwhelm rule your day.

- When you don't know what to do, start with the basics, formulate a plan, and keep moving toward your goal.

- Change in business can be a catalyst for innovation and growth. Learn from the mistakes of the past and push forward with humility and respect to improve the future.

- Technology should be thought of as a tool that works for the betterment of you and your business. Don't let technology become your master or distractor in life.

- When you feel as if you can't continue or you are beaten down, adopt the Viking mindset and push forward. You are much stronger then you realize.

ACKNOWLEDGMENTS

This journey to becoming the leader in my own life has been a true transformation. In every step there have been challenges and, after much determination, triumph. Through all of this my husband has continued to lean in with me. We have been determined to show our boys a real-life love story—one where life is never perfect but there is maximal effort given daily, to build a home where they learn the value of roots and wings. For this I am grateful beyond words.

The love and commitment that have been given to me have allowed me to challenge myself and continue to strive for more than I thought was possible the day before.

The extraordinary joys in my life are my children. My two young sons are the drivers of everything amazing that I do in my life. I have learned so much about myself as I learn the intricacies of being a mother. Although I have had my challenges due to illness, I have found strength in my responsibility to model health and wellness for them. Their love and kindness are a constant encouragement in my life, and these gifts have spurred me on to complete my goals. I am so grateful for each of them with their individual personalities and strengths.

Some people in life have a profound impact on you that you don't realize in the moment. The last few years have been filled with growth and memories. These memories have allowed me to be thankful for the time that I had with my grandparents. Their unwavering love and devotion, the discipline and values that they modeled throughout their lives. I realize now the impact they had on my development as a leader. I am grateful for all of their wisdom and mentorship that they imparted to me with love and generosity.

To my parents who continue to support our family with love and babysitting. The support and knowing that my children are enjoying such an amazing connection to their grandparents fills me with happiness.

I also thank all of the amazing paramedics and EMTs that I had the pleasure of serving with during my career. To the men and women who forged the way for the progression of paramedicine. To the women who stood tall in a male-dominated field and said that we belong. I am proud to have served with such outstanding first responders.

ABOUT THE AUTHOR

Christine Matzen is a medic at heart and worked in Emergency Medical Services for seventeen years in California, where she developed strong instincts and leadership skills as a paramedic. Working in such a fast-paced, high-stakes career gave her a deep intuition and respect for people.

She continued her education in business marketing and obtained her master's degree in leadership and management from Western Governors University. She is committed to helping people become leaders worth following. Her passion is helping leaders develop the skills and mindset that inspire people and cultivate true followers. She believes that leadership begins at every level and is the tone of an organization, home, and everyday life.

Christine is a wife and mother striving for excellence and learning as she goes. She lives in Texas with her family.